"Research shows that people perform their best and innovate the most when they feel excited and challenged. *Glow* is a provocative and insightful guidebook to engagement that will help you ignite your future."

—Richard Boyatzis, Professor in the Departments of Organizational Behavior, Psychology and Cognitive Science, Case Western Reserve University, and coauthor of *Primal Leadership: Learning to Lead with Emotional Intelligence* and *Resonant Leadership: Renewing Yourself and Connecting with Others Through Mindfulness, Hope, and Compassion*

"I chose to work in HR because I feel that it is very important to try to help other people to get a better life. Lynda Gratton is making a great contribution to this good cause with *Glow*. I encourage everyone to read it who wants a more meaningful life or to help others to achieve one."

—Hallstein Moerk, Executive Vice President, Human Resources, Nokia

"Warm and encouraging, Lynda lays out a wise path for living well in today's connected, global world. For young adults, *Glow*'s practical examples translate skills from your personal life into a rewarding work experience. For older adults concerned about remaining viable in a changing world, the book's thoughtful tools and reassuring themes provide the confidence for continued success."

—Tamara Erickson, author of *Plugged In: The Generation Y Guide to Thriving at Work* and *Retire Retirement: Career Strategies for the Boomer Generation*

FT Prentice Hall
FINANCIAL TIMES

In an increasingly competitive world, we believe it's quality of thinking that gives you the edge – an idea that opens new doors, a technique that solves a problem, or an insight that simply makes sense of it all. The more you know, the smarter and faster you can go.

That's why we work with the best minds in business and finance to bring cutting-edge thinking and best learning practice to a global market.

Under a range of leading imprints, including *Financial Times Prentice Hall*, we create world-class print publications and electronic products bringing our readers knowledge, skills and understanding, which can be applied whether studying or at work.

To find out more about Pearson Education publications, or tell us about the books you'd like to find, you can visit us at
www.pearsoned.co.uk

PEARSON
Education

Glow

How You Can Radiate Energy,
Innovation and Success

Lynda Gratton

 Prentice Hall

FINANCIAL TIMES

An imprint of **Pearson Education**

Harlow, England • London • New York • Boston • San Francisco • Toronto
Sydney • Tokyo • Singapore • Hong Kong • Seoul • Taipei • New Delhi
Cape Town • Madrid • Mexico City • Amsterdam • Munich • Paris • Milan

PEARSON EDUCATION LIMITED

Edinburgh Gate
Harlow CM20 2JE
Tel: +44 (0)1279 623623
Fax: +44 (0)1279 431059
Website: www.pearsoned.co.uk

First published in North America by Berrett-Koehler Publishers Inc., San Francisco 2009

First published in Great Britain 2009

ISBN: 978-0-273-72387-5

British Library Cataloguing-in-Publication Data
A catalogue record for this book is available from the British Library

10 9 8 7 6 5 4 3 2 1
13 12 11 10 09

Typeset in 12pt Arno Pro Light Display by 3
Printed and bound in Great Britain by Ashford Colour Press Ltd, Gosport

Interior design: Jonathan Peck, Dovetail Publishing Services.

The publisher's policy is to use paper manufactured from sustainable forests.

This book is dedicated to my sons,

Christian and Dominic,

with the heartfelt hope that they

can learn how to *Glow*.

Contents

Preface

As I see my children and students grow and take their place in the working world, I am increasingly driven by a vision of people at work *Glowing*. By this I mean that they radiate positive energy—are able to excite and ignite others and through their inspiration and innovation are able to create superior value and success in the workplace.

This is crucial. Work increasingly is how we define ourselves—it's what we spend the majority of our lives engaged in—whether we are men or women, Gen Y or baby boomers. It's what we do when we get up in the morning and often what's on our mind when our head hits the pillow at night. Don't get me wrong—I am not arguing for a total absorption in the world of work—but I do believe that each one of us deserves to live a fulfilling work life, to *Glow* ourselves and to see others *Glow*. Supporting people in organizations to create fulfilling work and innovative performance has been my overriding mission for the past twenty years.

I have written this book for everyone who strives to be more energized and innovative at work—characteristics I believe to be increasingly important to "staying ahead of the curve."

You could be just finishing your studies and wondering which path to take, midcareer and thinking about reenergizing, or like me a baby boomer considering how best to use my remaining decades of work.

There are two aspects of this book that I believe make it special and worth giving up your time to read and think about. First, it's based on deep research into what energized and innovative people actually do, so the three principles I describe later are ones that will really help you in your working life. Second, it addresses you as a person in the context of your work. This is important, for I have repeatedly seen people wanting to change but being surrounded by colleagues and situations that work against their changing. In this book you will discover how you can learn to *Glow*—but also what it would take for you to influence your immediate colleagues and the wider business or community that you work in.

In developing the ideas in this book I have used my own training as a psychologist and experience of coaching people to be more energized, innovative, and successful. I have also engaged with companies across the world to distinguish between places where energy flourishes and those that are moribund or, worse still, caught in the Big Freeze. Examining nearly two dozen companies in Europe, the United States, and Asia, my colleagues and I have built up a significant data set using state-of-the-art survey methodologies and computer analyses. What we have found is that there are indeed factors that separate the highly energized from the mundane—factors such as the way the company is structured, the behavior of senior executives, the cultivation of trust, and the pathways of network development. I described these factors in *Hot Spots: Why Some Companies Buzz with Energy and Innovation—and Others Don't,* published in 2007, illustrating what it would take for organizations to become places of energy and innovation.

As my colleagues and I began to follow up on the themes of *Hot Spots,* what became increasingly obvious was that high energy and innovation were not simply leveraged by the company. I began to see people who made a real difference through their behavior, competencies, and skills. So I began to ask, "What would it take for a person to really *Glow* with energy and innovation?"

What I discovered is that people who *Glow* had mastered three distinct areas of their life:

- They *Glow* because they have built deeply trusting and cooperative relationships with others.

- They *Glow* because they have extended their networks beyond the obvious to encompass the unusual.

- They *Glow* because they are on an inner quest that ignites their own energy and that of others.

To master these three distinct areas of their working life, people who *Glow* are adept at understanding what they have to do as individuals, what they have to do as members of a team, and how to find their place in a company that encourages them to *Glow*.

These are significant areas of life to master, and so my challenge in this book is to use the examples I have seen to blaze a path that will encourage you to master these three areas in a way that is as elegantly simple as possible. I hope you will see this simplicity in the examples, the profile, and the action points I present. My aim is to engage and inspire you without overburdening you. In the interests of simplicity, I made three decisions about this book. First, there are no references to other people's research or theories except where I have used direct quotes. Instead, I have made reference to others' work in the Recommended Reading section at the back of the book, where you may find more information on themes you would like to pursue. Second, I make little reference to my own research, which frames this book, for complete information on that is available at http://www.hotspotsmovement.com. Third, I have tried to focus your attention on the key issues through a simple diagnostic profile I have developed. This is designed to help you understand where you stand with regard to your own attitudes and competencies, your team, and your organization. The profile is included in this book, but you may also download a copy from http://www.hotspotsmovement.com where you will also find the *Glow* Checklist.

Writing this book has been a hugely enjoyable and inspiring task, not least because I have had to look at myself in a way that I have not before. Working with me on this task have been some truly *Glowing* people. In particular I would like to thank my editors at Berrett-Koehler and FT Prentice Hall. This is the second book I have produced with Steve Piersanti, Richard Stagg, and Liz Gooster, and again the experience has been terrific. I have also discovered that in writing a book for a particular audience, my reviewers have been particularly helpful and insightful. I would like thank Stuart Emery, Faith Gibson, John Hughes, Judith Leary Joyce, Jeffrey Kulick, Christopher Morris, Danielle Scott and Irene Sitbon.

I launched the Hot Spots Movement in September 2007 in order to gain more traction on the topic of individual and organizational energy and innovation. Working with the core team—Andreas Voigt, Marilyn Davison, Johanna Walker, and Talie Wood—has been a wonderful experience. Thanks in particular to Andreas Voigt for the passion he brings to this subject.

On a balmy evening in summer 2008, more than fifty people gathered in a secret garden in central London to support the aims of the movement and to lend their goodwill and grace to it. Our band of well-wishers has become an increasingly important community—as have the many thousands of people across the world who have lent their interest and encouragement.

I believe it is possible for each one of us to become more inspiring and innovative in our work—to truly *Glow*. This book is an invitation to the journey and a heartfelt plea for more humane and engaging work. We deserve it ourselves—and owe it as our legacy to those who come after us. We all benefit when jobs and lives *Glow*.

Chapter One

The Secrets of Glowing

You only have to glance at the morning paper to read that globalization marches on, and technology continuously changes the way you work. The result? There is always someone, somewhere in the world, who will volunteer to do your work faster, quicker, and cheaper. So where does this leave you?

In an ever-changing world, how can you be sure that you will find and pursue great opportunities? How can you ensure that you stay fresh and energized? What will it take for you to become the first person of call when an exciting assignment comes along? How can you relentlessly create value in your work and for yourself? How will you stay ahead of the curve?

Staying Ahead of the Curve

These are everyday questions that you and I and everyone around us must ask ourselves on a fairly frequent basis. It does not matter where you are in your career. You could be fresh out of college and wondering where to go next. You could be in the midst of your career and thinking about how to become more innovative. Or you could be contemplating the final years of your working life and wondering how to stay engaged and energized. Wherever you are in your work life, you want to be sure you stay ahead of the curve.

Fall short in any way, and globalization gobbles you up. Around the world, someone, somewhere, has already put in a bid to do it faster, quicker, and cheaper. To stay ahead of the curve, you have to work with more energy, more enthusiasm, and most important of all, more innovation. It is this combination that will bring you long-term success in this globalized, technology-enabled world.

But how do you do this without becoming yet another victim of an "extreme job"—working harder and harder just to keep up, your health in jeopardy, alienating your family and friends, and moving further and further away from your true self?

When You Glow

Over the last couple of decades I have watched people who manage to stay ahead of the curve—people who are energized, innovative, and successful—and yet remain healthy and happy. I have interviewed them in their offices, I have watched them as they work, and I have studied them in their teams.

What strikes me as I watch them is that they seem to *Glow*. You can see it in their faces; you can hear it in their voices. They radiate positive energy that has the effect of inspiring others, attracting interesting work, and creating amazing relationships and networks. Think about your own circle of friends and acquaintances. Do you know some people who *Glow*? Do you know others who always seem to be in a perpetual state of Big Freeze?

I am trained as a psychologist, so when I first tried to puzzle out why some people *Glow* and others don't, I thought it was a personality trait. Maybe some people are born to *Glow* and others aren't. But I soon discovered that people with all sorts of different personalities could *Glow*. What I found is that people who *Glow* have something in common, and it's not their personality.

You *Glow* when you radiate positive energy—that fosters a great working experience for yourself, excites and ignites others, and through your inspiration and innovation creates superior value and success in your work.

All of us have moments when we feel we are *Glowing*. It could be when a project goes particularly well or when working with a colleague feels especially rewarding or when suddenly someone you barely know comes up with an idea for a problem that has been on your mind for ages. It is at these times that you feel great about what you are doing, times when working with others has never seemed more natural, times when you really feel part of something bigger—times when you feel really successful.

When you radiate this positive energy, great things happen to you. When you *Glow*, you are able to create or find and flourish in what I call Hot Spots.

- *Glowing* is something that happens to you and involves your radiating energy and innovation.

- Hot Spots are times, places, and occasions when whole groups or a community of people become highly energized and innovative.

So your challenge is to learn how to *Glow* and then to create, find, and flourish in Hot Spots.

Glowing Every Day

The challenge is that sometimes the very actions you think will make you indispensable are exactly those that make you disposable.

I see examples every day of people taking what they sincerely believe to be the best course of action to create value for themselves and others, yet instead of *Glowing* and creating or finding a Hot Spot, they are inadvertently behaving in ways and creating situations that reduce their value and leave them devoid of energy and unattractive to others.

How Fred Becomes Disposable

Fred has been in his company for five years and really wants to succeed. One day his manager gives Fred a tough piece of work to do. It really tests the limits of Fred's competence, but he is delighted to have the opportunity. Faced with this tough task, here is what Fred does:

1. First, he decides to "put his head down" so he can really concentrate on the task at hand.

2. Then he decides to close his office door so that he will not be disturbed and to reduce the temptation of wandering around and being distracted by others.

3. Then he increases his working hours and stays late into the evening in order to meet the tough deadline.

4. Finally, Fred works on the task all by himself to make sure that his boss will realize just how indispensable he is.

Sound familiar? That's the position many of us would take. Faced with a tough assignment, you hunker down, concentrate, and reduce what you perceive as distractions, and try to do it yourself. It's one of the reasons work becomes extreme—as people like Fred try to stay ahead of the curve by working longer and longer hours.

Fred's not stupid. He behaves as he does because he assumes that what he is doing will help him stay ahead of the curve. So what was in Fred's mind when he took this course of action? This is what he told me:

I have the answers, so I need to really concentrate to get them out of my head. . . . Others will be a distraction—so I need to reduce my interactions with other people to ensure I can really concentrate. . . . Working long hours will increase my productivity and be the key to success.

What Fred had forgotten was that there is always someone, somewhere, who is eager to do it faster, quicker, and cheaper—and work even longer hours.

So what happens to Fred? Over time his assumptions about how to outperform others and the actions he takes leave him drained and deenergized. He's put all his energy into getting through the task and arrives home every night bad-tempered and irritable. His headaches become so bothersome that he arranges to see a doctor, who tells him they are stress-related.

Fred does not become disposable because of his headaches (although they did not help). He is disposable because he is failing to add significant value to the project. Yes, he is working harder and working longer hours. But what he was not doing was working with flair. Fred failed to add value because he failed to bring enthusiasm and innovation to the project.

Over time Fred discovered that rather than enjoying the task, he was entering what I call the Big Freeze, a time when energy is drained and innovation ceases.

By closing in on himself, Fred has inadvertently violated the very principles that would keep him energized, increase his value, and ensure that he stays ahead of the curve by being innovative. To understand what these principles may be, let's turn to Frank, who takes a rather different approach than Fred did.

How Frank Stays Ahead of the Curve

When Frank's manager gives him a tough piece of work to do, here is what Frank does:

1. First, he turns to colleagues he trusts and who trust him and asks them for advice and insight into the problem.

2. Then he reaches out into his extended network to find others who have faced similar problems and to discover what they have actually done.

3. He also redefines the problem in such a way that it ignites others' interest and enthusiasm and injects energy and innovation into the community.

The result is that Frank exceeds others' expectations because he is able to bring innovation and flair to the project.

You can see that Frank takes a completely different approach than Fred. Clearly, he has a different set of assumptions in mind about how the work should be done. When I quizzed Frank about his way of working, this is what he said:

I know I don't have all the answers, so I really need others to cooperate with me to solve this tricky project. I want my solution to be as innovative as possible.... It's important to me that I reach out to people I know who have some knowledge in this field to give me insights. But I also realize that people who are very different from me may also have an interesting angle, so I try to spend time with a wider circle of acquaintances.... For me, the most important key to success is to create an idea or a task that others are drawn to so we can solve it together.

By opening up, Frank begins to take actions that energized, high-value, innovative, and ultimately indispensable people take. People like Frank *Glow*.

You hear it in their positive, upbeat attitude toward life, you feel it in their warmth and emotional connectivity, and you see it in the way they connect with others, build networks, and engage with inspiring questions. People who *Glow* have a huge advantage over the Freds of this world. When you *Glow*, people feel good about you; they want to be around you, they want to be part of what you are doing, they want you to succeed, and they become your loyal supporters.

I must admit, however, the sad truth is that much of the time, you are more likely to have Fred's experiences than Frank's. My research has shown that the majority of people feel energized, engaged, and innovative less than 20 percent of their working lives. What a terrible waste.

As you can see in Fred's story, this is not because Fred is lazy, stupid, or incompetent. Far from it. And you, like Fred, do the very best you can. The problem is that the way you think about your work—your assumptions about what makes for success and the habits and skills you develop—can inadvertently push you into the Big Freeze rather than encourage and enable you to *Glow*.

For a couple of decades now I have been fascinated by the Big Freeze, where Fred has found himself—and in people like Frank who have instead taken a path that taught them to *Glow*. My research projects have helped me understand what it is that people like Frank actually do. I have also tried to apply these principles to my own working life so that I might understand what it takes and feel some of the challenges and opportunities that come when you strive to *Glow*.

In this book you will discover a whole host of people who, like Frank, have learned what it takes to *Glow* and have translated this understanding into their day-to-day actions. I will share some of my own experiences and insights as I have tried to *Glow* in my own working life. You will find insights, tools, and techniques that will help you *Glow*—and thus create a working environment that you feel really, really good about. Isn't that what you deserve for your efforts?

And it's more than just a reward. The truth is that the Big Freeze that Fred experiences doesn't just affect his performance on the job. It also affects his health—his headaches tell you that he is more likely to suffer from all sorts of stress-related diseases. It also affects his family and friends when he comes home tired and bad-tempered and disinclined to engage with the people around him. And of course it affects his long-term prospects. As Fred gets deeper into the cycle of the Big Freeze, he begins to lose his value and become less successful. He doesn't develop new skills, fails to make important connections, and over time depletes his personal capital. So when opportunities come along, Fred is the last to be offered them.

I'd like to make one last point about Fred and Frank. When you think about their story, perhaps you regard it as a tale about how one person learned to *Glow* and the other found himself in the Big Freeze. Certainly, their attitudes, skills, and habits played an important role in their success or failure at staying ahead of the curve. But this is not simply a story about two men alone in the working world. Like you, Fred and Frank are part of a larger group of people—a team, a company, a community—and they are also part of wider business networks and informal networks of suppliers and clients and contacts. So one of the reasons Frank stays ahead of the curve is because of the way he works with the people around him and the choices he makes about those he works with.

For example, Frank cannot be cooperative unless the people around him are willing to cooperate with him. It takes two hands to clap! And Frank cannot reach out to a wider network if those around him discourage him from doing so. Frank is a resource himself, but his immediate colleagues and team are also a resource, and so is the network in which he works.

The implications of this are that although there are actions Fred can take by himself, many of the actions he takes are the result of the wider context of his life and work. (We will be returning to this wider context after looking more deeply at what it takes to *Glow*.)

When I observed and interviewed people like Frank who *Glow*, I discovered that people like Frank live life according to three principles that form the foundation for their daily behavior. These principles are brought to life every day by nine actions. Together these principles and actions create a frame for their work life that stokes their enthusiasm and enables them to *Glow*.

The Three Principles That Are the Foundation of Glowing

People like Frank approach their working lives by applying three broad principles: a cooperative mindset, jumping across worlds, and igniting latent energy.

The First Principle: A Cooperative Mindset

Recall that the first action Frank took when faced with a tough problem was to reach out to others—and his colleagues responded positively to him and were willing and enthusiastic in their support of him. This sort of interaction is not a one-off event. For Frank, this approach is part of his deeply held beliefs about others and is also the result of skills and habits he has polished over time. Frank is able to reach out because he has a warm and positive attitude toward others. In his working life, he reinforces this by generally choosing to work in places where he knows cooperation flourishes. Frank has also over time developed great conversational and relationship skills and habits that enable him to establish high-quality connections with others. These relationships bring him great pleasure both on the job and away from work.

Three actions support the principle of cooperation. The first is the development of habits and skills of cooperation. The second is becoming adept at listening to others and engaging in good conversations with others. The third is taking action around where and with whom you work. This may seem like an unusual action to be considering with regard to cooperation. But recall that Frank worked with people who were prepared to support him when he needed help. He knew he could reach out to them because he had helped cultivate a cooperative environment; the flip side of that coin is that in the past he had made conscious decisions to leave places where cooperation was limited and to move to his current job, where cooperation flourished. That does not mean, by the way, that you should leave your job immediately if the climate isn't right. What it does mean is that the next time you have an opportunity to accept a project, take a new job, or join a different company, you will want to ensure that cooperation will thrive in the new environment.

The Second Principle: Jumping Across Worlds

When Frank faced a difficult task, he reached out into his extended network to find other people who had faced similar problems. Recall that in the face of a similar task, Fred hunkered down and closed in on himself, whereas Frank opened up to others. Frank knew that in his wider circle, there could be people who offer another point of view or a new way of looking at the problem. This reaching out—particularly to people who are different—will be crucial to your capacity to *Glow* and to innovate in your work. And to meet people who are different, you must be prepared to jump across the boundary that surrounds you—the boundary that perhaps separates your part of the business from another part—into other worlds or across age groups and nationalities. The fresh perceptions that come from jumping across worlds will be crucial to your capacity to remain excited and innovative—to *Glow*.

This sounds like a major change from your standard everyday existence. So how will you implement this principle on a daily basis? I'll tell you what I have found. People who are good at jumping across worlds place a high value on their network and know precisely what their network is doing for them. They also take action to increase the value of their network by seizing the right opportunities to jump the boundaries. They make sure that when innovation is important, they have access to people who are different and can bring fresh perspectives and insights.

Just as important as cooperation in the place you work is your capacity to jump across worlds. There are workplaces where huge walls around everything make it almost impossible for you to jump over them. There are other places where great pathways between functions or businesses or age groups that you can easily tap into are already thriving. People like Frank who *Glow* are aware of this and are very careful to understand what a company or team is like before joining. Are the walls unscalable, or are they just the right height for jumping?

The Third Principle: Igniting Latent Energy

When Frank thought about how to proceed in his work, he knew that bringing other people in could be a great source of innovation. But how would he attract them to work with him? All the talented people around him already have plenty of work on their plate; why would they agree to cooperate with him? Part of the reason, of course, is that by practicing the first two principles, Frank has created a feeling of goodwill around him. But that's not enough. What he also needs to do is to entice and excite people.

When, like Frank, you learn the habits and skills of cooperation and have become adept at jumping across worlds, you create what I call latent energy. By that I mean that you have generated within yourself and in your immediate community the potential to become really energized. However, if you want to make use of this potential or latent energy, you need to be adept sparking it with some form of ignition, for only when latent energy is ignited can it deliver the excitement and innovation that are so crucial to *Glowing*. Three actions support the principle of igniting latent energy. The first is to ask questions that spark energy, to engross and interest others' as well as you own curiosity—questions like "how can we fundamentally change our customer experience?" to bigger questions like "How could we make a real difference in our community?" to truly enormous questions like "What does this mean for world hunger?" The second action is to create visions that compel. These are visions of the future that you and your colleagues can buy into, that encourage others to imagine the future and to become excited about being involved in that future. The third action you can take is to work with others to craft meaningful and exciting work.

Glowing is about living these three principles. You live them through skills, habits, and choices that reflect these principles and weave them into your day-to-day experiences.

The Nine Actions That Will Make You Glow Every Day

Let's now pull the nine actions together—three in support of each principle—and take a closer look at what you have to do to significantly increase your personal happiness and your capacity to build your personal value through innovation and energy.

Actions That Support the First Principle, a Cooperative Mindset

Action 1   People who *Glow* have positive ways of thinking about others and five *daily habits of cooperation*. They have realistic and positive expectations of others and are prepared to share valuable information with others, to act with discretion, to use the language of cooperation, and to make and keep commitments.

Action 2   People who *Glow* know the *art of great conversation*, and use conversation as the bedrock of their cooperation with others. They are able to bring emotional authenticity and analytical rigor to their conversations.

Action 3   People who *Glow* are astute at acting on the *"smell of the place."* They know the signs of the Big Freeze and how to avoid them and take action to ensure that they move to teams and communities where cooperation flourishes.

☀ Actions That Support the Second Principle, Jumping Across Worlds

Action 4   People who *Glow* are *skilled at increasing the value of their networks* and at balancing their networks between acquaintances and close friends who are similar to them with more extensive networks of people who are very different from them. They know that sometimes the most interesting and most innovative ideas come from people whom they barely know and who are very different from them.

Action 5   People who *Glow* have *broad and extensive networks* and are skilled at escaping the boundaries that constrain them. They allow for serendipity in their life and are prepared to meet new people and take untrodden paths to broaden their experiences.

Action 6   People who *Glow* are adept at *finding and moving to boundaryless places*. They know how to escape from the Fortress and connect with teams and places that encourage them to grow by creating opportunities to jump across worlds.

☀ Actions That Support the Third Principle, Igniting Latent Energy

Action 7   People who *Glow* are adept at asking the big questions that spark energy, which requires courage and focus.

Action 8   People who *Glow* are able to create a compelling vision that sparks energy and is so exciting and engaging that others are drawn to it.

Action 9   People who *Glow* are able to craft meaningful and exciting work that stimulates them and others.

These nine actions will ensure that you stay ahead of the curve and are more likely to find yourself *Glowing* than in the Big Freeze. In Chapter Two you will discover the resources that will help you *Glow*.

Key Points in Chapter One

The Secrets of *Glowing*

In this ever-changing world, you must stay ahead of the curve and be the first point of call when new opportunities arise.

You do this by *Glowing*—by radiating positive energy that fosters a great working experience for yourself, that excites and ignites others through your inspiration, and that reflects the innovation and enthusiasm that deliver superior value in your work.

The challenge is that sometimes the very actions you think will make you indispensable are exactly those that make you disposable. You forget that there is always someone, somewhere, who will do it faster, quicker, and cheaper.

When you *Glow*, you design your working life around three principles:

The First Principle: A Cooperative Mindset
You have a warm and positive attitude toward others and choose to work where cooperation flourishes. You have developed conversational and relationship skills and habits.

The Second Principle: Jumping Across Worlds
You have jumped across into other worlds and have learned to appreciate and learn from people who are very different from you.

The Third Principle: Igniting Latent Energy
You are able to ignite your own energy and the energy of those around you by discovering sources of ignition.

You live these principles on a daily basis through nine actions:

Action 1   You practice the daily habits of cooperation.

Action 2   You master the art of great conversation.

Action 3   You act on the "smell of the place."

Action 4   You know how to increase the value of your network.

Action 5   You are skilled at escaping the boundaries that constrain you.

Action 6   You find and move to boundaryless places.

Action 7   You ask questions that spark energy.

Action 8   You create visions that compel.

Action 9   You craft meaningful and exciting work.

Chapter Two

Your Glow Resources

You want to make *Glowing* a daily experience in your working life rather than something that happens occasionally. You do this by working on the three principles defined in Chapter One and developing your skills and competencies in the nine actions described there.

Stop for a moment and think—does this seem like tall an order? Too many actions for you to take right now? Possibly it does. But before you feel truly overwhelmed, remember that in building your skills and creating more value in your working life, you have three potential resources available to you. Think carefully about each of these resources and how they could be of service to you.

☀ The Potential Resources That Make Glowing a Daily Experience

1. Your first resource is yourself. You have within you the power to develop the personal skills and capabilities that are the foundation for a life of *Glowing*.

2. Your second resource is your team, your immediate colleagues—they can play a key role in supporting and enabling you and other team members to practice the nine actions that will ensure that you *Glow*.

3. Your third resource is the community, business, or organization in which you currently work. Even if you work completely on your

own, you are a member of a wider community of people who can provide a frame for you to develop these skills and habits. If you are a member of a small business or a large organization, this can also be a crucial resource to ensure that you *Glow*.

In the stories that follow, you will meet people who have been able to use these three resources for support, encouragement, and skill development. You will also meet people who are in teams or communities that have significantly narrowed their opportunities and limited their choices. These resources can provide a wonderful support to *Glowing*—but they can also act as a serious barrier.

So it is wise for you to understand where you stand with regard to each of these resources. Are these three potential resources supporting you to *Glow*, or are they barriers? Once you have figured this out, it will be clearer to you whether you need to build on their support or reduce the barriers.

To help you to do this, you can use a short diagnostic—the *Glow* Profile (introduced toward the end of this chapter). This profile enables you to quickly and accurately identify whether the three resources available to you (yourself; your team; and your community, business, or organization) are supporting you on the path to *Glowing* or reducing your opportunities. Once you know where you stand right now, you are in a better position to decide how you will focus the development of your skills and resources.

So take a closer look at these three resources to understand more deeply how they can act as a resource for you.

You as a Potential Resource: Glowing from the Inside

Glowing every day starts with you. Your attitudes and assumptions make a difference (think back to Fred's assumptions and how that narrowed his *Glow* experiences), and so do the skills and habits you choose to develop.

The resources you have to make *Glowing* a daily experience include the following:

- Your assumptions and attitudes about your work and your colleagues

- Your capacity to be authentic and to build trust with others

- The habits you choose to develop

- The alternatives you see and the choices you make about your work

- The talents and capabilities you decide to develop

- The type of people you decide to spend your time with at work and outside of work

So you have to think carefully about the way you look at the world, the choices you make, and the skills and habits you focus on developing. You can be your own greatest supporter—or your own worst enemy!

The way you look at the world and the actions you take have a profound impact on your capacity to *Glow*. My suggestion here is that you leverage your personal style by looking more closely at the aspects of your natural personality that you want to accentuate and amplify.

Your personality, style, and competencies are important resources to you. But as Frank found, being able to *Glow* is not simply about you as a person, isolated from others. It's about your relationship with others and ultimately about the team and community with whom you work.

Your Team as a Potential Resource: Glowing with Your Colleagues

Ultimately, your capacity to *Glow* is up to you. But you flourish because of the people you are with. They can help you feel great and energized—or they can sap your energy and creativity. Recall that Frank was able to call on the people around him to ensure that he could deliver high-quality and innovative results, whereas Fred found himself increasingly isolated.

Your colleagues and team can give you the support, the insight, and the knowledge that will ensure that you *Glow* and stay ahead of the curve. They can also be the catalysts for the cold winds of the Big Freeze to blow around your ankles!

We all work in different ways, so what you think of as a "team" may not be the same as someone else's. If you work independently, your team will be your immediate colleagues and soul mates and also your suppliers or clients. If you work in a commercial business, your team will be the project teams and task forces you work with. If you work for a not-for-profit organization, your team will be the people you serve and the others you engage with. No one works in complete isolation.

Your capacity to make use of these potentially wonderful resources is dependent in part on the way you interact and on your own and your colleagues' attitudes, skills, and habits. Indeed, your capacity to reach out to those around you to become a resource depends on a variety of things:

- Your attitudes and behavior toward your colleagues

- The extent to which your colleagues are prepared to cooperate with each other and with you

- The way your colleagues work with people outside the immediate team

- The extent to which you and your colleagues are prepared to confront important questions and issues

- Whether you can encourage your team or colleagues to support you in your vision of the future

So you have to think about what sort of team or colleagues you should be working with and whether your current team members are in fact able to support you and, if they cannot, what you need to do to gain their support.

The key message here is that your team is crucial to you, and you can influence the extent to which team members support you by the way you behave toward them and even by choosing to remain with them over the longer term (more on this later).

Your Business as a Potential Resource: Glowing in Your Extended Community

The third resource available to you to ensure that you *Glow* is the business or community that surrounds you. Even if you work independently, your extended community and networks of people can be a crucial resources.

Be it an informal support network or a large business, your extended community can be a valuable resource because it provides opportunities for Hot Spots to arise. Your extended community can also drain you of energy and enthusiasm.

Of course, you may feel that you have very little influence over your business or community. However, as I will show you, there are ways you can influence your wider environment—from the way you decide to interact with others and the choices you make to deciding that this is not a business or community you want to be a member of.

The reason why your extended community is such a crucial potential resource is that it is within this wider community that Hot Spots are likely to flare up, and these provide wonderful opportunities for you to *Glow*. As noted in Chapter One, Hot Spots are times, places, and occasions when your latent energy and that of others is suddenly ignited in the service of some greater goal. In an informal network the goal could be the creation of something exciting and new—in the way that Wikipedia and Linux are extraordinary communities that have created Hot Spots of innovation and productivity. Or this could happen in a company—in the way that the Nano car was the focus of a Hot Spot that burned for four years in the Tata Group in India.

So where you work and the network you are part of can make a big difference in whether you *Glow* or not. There are some workplaces that inspire you and are natural creators of Hot Spots. There are other places where you are more likely to encounter the Big Freeze. In your workplace, whether you *Glow* or not is influenced by a number of things:

- Whether the role models and leaders in your extended community behave in a cooperative way

- Your day-to-day experience of your work and the habits and routines of people around you—for example, how people routinely communicate with each other, how people are selected to join the community or business, and how resources are allocated among people

- Whether your business or community has networks that extend out to well-wishers and supporters

- The extent to which the business or wider community encourages and supports you personally to widen your networks of friends and associates

- Whether you are encouraged to pursue friendships and contacts with people outside your immediate team

So you have to think carefully about the community, company, or business you join (and when to leave), the executives you work with, and the negotiations you make about the development of your skills.

You may be wondering why you should concentrate at all on the business or company you work for. Perhaps you see yourself as a very small cog in a very large wheel. You may feel that you have very little discretion over the way you work or indeed over the company you join. But the truth is, you are not powerless. Through your own will and volition, it is possible for you to change the context in which you work through the practices you support and encourage.

Even if you feel it will be tough to change the culture or values of the place, there are actions you can take. You can leave the business or company you are in right now if you feel that you are unlikely to encounter the Hot Spots of energy that will enable you to *Glow*. Or you can actively move from a part of the company that is devoid of hope to one that appears to be more vibrant.

You may be working for yourself with a couple of associates or for a medium-sized business or for a multinational company that has offices in different countries. You may still be in education and wondering how to make choices about what to do and where to work, or you may be already established or, like me, thinking about how to make the most of the next decade of work. Where you are in your career or the size of the company you join is not the deciding factor when it comes your finding Hot Spots or learning how to *Glow*. What is important is you.

You Can Glow—It's You That Makes It Happen

As you go through this book, you will deepen your understanding of the three principles and the nine actions that ensure that you stay ahead of the curve. Using the *Glow* Profile, you will calibrate the extent to which your potential resources (you, your team, and your business or community) are able to support you in making sure you *Glow* every day. The profile will also help you pinpoint where you can best take action. I will be on hand to give you ideas, tips, and stories that will energize and entertain you and show you how others (including myself) have made this work.

Tips on Learning to *Glow*

You can significantly increase your potential to *Glow*. A few basic tips will help you succeed.

Remember that it's not about your personality

Perhaps you believe you don't really have the personality that will really enable you to *Glow* every day. Perhaps you think you are too "introverted" or lack self-confidence or don't have a personality that attracts interesting, creative people to work with you. The problem with these self-doubts is that they can lead you to give up hope and settle for a working life that is more like the Big Freeze than a Hot Spot of energy and excitement.

The idea that there is a *Glow* "personality type" is a myth. What is important is that you learn to take the nine actions on a day-to-day basis. You can take these actions in your own way; there is no one type of person who is particularity adept at *Glowing*. You can be an introvert or an extrovert, a thinker or a feeler, highly intuitive or judgemental . . . and still *Glow*.

Use all your potential resources

What's really important are the actions and habits you—and only you—adopt. Some of these actions are big actions—like having the courage to ask igniting questions, which might not come up in your life that often. Others are day-to-day habits—like remembering to put time aside every day to have a significant conversation with one of your colleagues or taking a different route to work. Remember that of all the resources available to you, it is your will, your development, and your choices that will really make a difference.

This seems deceptively straightforward. Of course, you may be thinking, I'm the one who makes this happen. However, I have found that some people get the message about what *Glowing* is and where they stand and then fail to take action.

When people fail to take action, they typically concentrate on one resource but not all of them. Some fail to take action around themselves—they don't really question their own attitudes or strive to develop new habits and skills. Or they fail to take action in their team or networks and let these fester and become places where the Big Freeze creeps in. Others still do nothing about the place in which they work.

The marvelous thing about *Glowing*, of course, is that it is you who make it happen. It is your will, your choices, and your development that generate energy, happiness, and innovation. So you don't have to wait to be asked— you don't have to wait for someone else to start. You can start right now and get to work on the mindset and attitudes you have, the choices you make, the actions you take, and the habits you develop.

You have to explore the mindset you have. You have to think and feel your way into *Glowing*. In the sections that follow, I will take you through a number of thought exercises designed to help you frame your thinking about this.

Next, you have to examine the choices you make—for example, the people you choose to spend time with, the networks you choose to develop, the groups you work with, and the companies and businesses you join. For each of these choices, the *Glow* Profile will give you some pointers about where you are now and what you need to do.

Finally, you have to pay attention to the actions you take and the habits you develop. There are certain habits and behaviors that could make a real difference in your degree of energy, happiness and innovation—and ultimately your success. I will show you what these habits and behaviors are and the concrete actions you can take to develop them.

Yes, you can *Glow* if you concentrate on the way you think about the world, the choices you make, and the skills and habits you focus on developing.

Confront your pet theories about success

Finding places of high energy in which you can *Glow* is so wonderful and important to your success that you will want to re-create the experience again and again. Beware, though, that you don't simply try the same thing over and over and rely on pet theories rather than really understanding what it takes to *Glow* every day.

Let me give you an example by recounting the tale of the tribe and the pig. A long time ago in a distant land, there was a tribe of forest dwellers. One day, during a particularly vicious electrical storm, a bolt of lightning struck a tree under which a wild pig was sheltering. The poor creature was roasted alive by the blast. The smell and taste of the roasted pork was so enticing to the people of the tribe that they rushed to devour it with great enjoyment. In fact, they enjoyed it so much that from that day on, every time there was an electrical storm, the people caught a wild pig and tethered it to a tree, waiting for lightning to strike.

This almost certainly fictitious story nevertheless drives home the fact that when something marvelous and unexpected happens (like a roasted pig or a Hot Spot or that *Glowing* feeling), you tend to generalize from that single event and build a theory on it. These theories can be wrong. They can be too specific (for example, the tethering of the pig); they can fail to recognize the underlying factors (for example, that there are other ways of roasting pork); and they may rely on the recurrence of a low-probability event (that the same tree will again be struck by lightning).

Surely there have been times in your life when you have felt that you were *Glowing* or you experienced being in a Hot Spot. It might have been around certain people or in certain places or at certain times. So to re-create the feeling and experience, you go back over the same routes—finding the same people and hanging around in the same places. What you are overlooking is that there could be many other routes to *Glowing* and creating, finding, or flourishing in Hot Spots—with different people, in different places, and at different times.

Don't simply try to replicate the context that created Hot Spots for you in the past. In this book you will learn that there are many ways to *Glow* and many ways to find, create, and flourish in Hot Spots.

Work equally on all three principles

As noted earlier, people who *Glow* pursue their working lives on the basis of three principles. They are positive, collaborative and trusting with others; they enjoy jumping across worlds to meet people different from themselves; and they are questioning and capable of creating a meaningful and inspiring vision.

Staying ahead of the curve means working on all three principles. You will become frustrated by incapacity to really *Glow* if you only focus on one principle. For example, you work really hard on developing your habits around cooperation but then fail to bridge to others who are different from you. Or you work hard on widening your networks and bridge to people unlike you but then fail to find anything that ignites the latent energy in these networks.

Of course, it is only natural that you strive to develop those skills and attitudes at which you excel. So if you are warmhearted, you build cooperation, or if you are an easygoing networker, you concentrate on widening your networks. Or if you are a counterintuitive thinker, asking the igniting questions or envisioning meaningful tasks is second nature to you.

However, if you focus only on what comes most naturally, you may ignore other aspects that are just as important. The three principles work together in a cumulative, integrated way. To learn to *Glow*, you must make sure that you are giving each of the three principles equal focus and attention.

Find a work partner or a group to Glow with

Fred made the mistake of thinking that to stay ahead of the curve, he needed to keep his head down and work harder. Frank took the view that colleagues around him and his wider networks could support him.

The same is true for this project—the project to increase the amount of time you *Glow*. You could complete the *Glow* Profile and think about your actions completely on your own. The truth is that this is my natural course of action. I am an introvert (most writers are, by the way, even if they can put on a performance when required), so my sympathies lie with Fred. Faced with a problem (how to *Glow* more in my life), I am likely to hunker down and try to get through it myself.

But what I have learned over the years is that just as *Glowing* is about your relationships with others, learning to *Glow* is something you can embark on with others. So over the years I have called on a few friends for support. Sometimes it's explicit—one of my dearest friends, Dominic, is a Buddhist, so I look to him on occasion for a moral compass when discussing issues with him. Other times it has been spending time with people who have the positive and upbeat way of living that I would like to develop in myself. I was lucky to have a close friend in Sumantra Ghoshal (now sadly passed away); he was wonderful at acting as a mirror to me and how I was behaving.

The bottom line is that you can do this on your own, but it may be both instructive and fun to involve others. You can ask your friends and colleagues to take a look at this book and complete the profile for how they see you (and in the spirit of cooperation, you can complete the profile for them). They can help you recognize your blind spots—aspects of yourself that you are unaware of. For example, it was Sumantra who pointed out to me that most of my close friends are very similar to me in terms of education, lifestyle, and beliefs. As soon as he told me this, I realized he was right—but I had never noticed it myself; it was a real blind spot. I immediately saw that I was failing to jump across worlds because I spent too much time with people very similar to myself.

Your friends and colleagues may also identify positive aspects of yourself that you had not really recognized or had underestimated. These friends can also draw your attention to aspects of yourself that they really value but perhaps you take for granted—and of course you can do the same for them.

So talking with others would be a wonderful opportunity for both you and them to learn to *Glow* more. As you think about how you might best support one another, here are some ground rules you may find useful to share:

Find people who are also excited. Take the initiative—give your colleagues a copy of this book, and ask them to work with you. Try to find people who have a positive outlook, who care about you (and whom you care about), who have enough time to engage in conversation with you, and who are potentially different enough from you to bring a fresh perspective.

Make sure everyone gets equal amounts of air time. Inevitably, some colleagues will be more talkative and extroverted than others. So the temptation is for them to talk more and more and the introverts to talk less and less. Giving equal airtime is crucial if your helpmates are to stay together and flourish. It may be wise, at least the beginning, to allocate a certain amount of time to each person and stick to this time allocation.

Listen, listen, listen. You know the feeling: you are talking and you can see that the person with you is thinking of other things and is simply waiting for you to stop so that he or she can jump in. Make it clear that listening is crucial to a supportive community like this—so be conscious of this and as a group monitor how well you are at listening to one another.

Don't get defensive. If your colleagues are working well together, they will be revealing and discussing blind spots—positive aspects of yourself you undervalued or negative things you really did not know about yourself. I recall how upset I was when a dear friend told me that I can sound harsh at times. I checked it out—"Do I sometimes sound judgmental and harsh?" I asked my sister Heather. "Of course!" she replied. I should have realized this, but I did not. I guess I thought I was being helpful. But it didn't come across that way, and that was something I had to work on if I was to honor the principle of cooperation and learn to *Glow* more of the time.

I have heard people say the same about blind spots—that when negatives are brought to the surface, they can be difficult to comprehend. I guess if they were easy to comprehend, they would not be in your blind spot. So as members of a learning community, try not to become defensive when negatives surface. It is often at these difficult moments that true learning takes place.

You will find that others can be a useful resource for creating an atmosphere of learning, awareness, insight, and courage.

Forget the myth of patience

Sometimes you feel powerless, that there is nothing you can do, that life will take its course. That if you wait long enough, you will eventually *Glow* and find a Hot Spot. This is the myth of patience. You don't have to wait—you can take action now that will ensure that you *Glow* every day of your life.

I have some sympathy for the myth of waiting. Certainly there have been times in my life when I have felt that I was working in a Big Freeze and that there was really nothing I could do. At such times, I feel overwhelmed by the negative energy and angry at my own impotence. These are times when I feel that my work and I have drifted apart, that I have lost control of what I am at work or how I work. I am a natural optimist and always believe that, despite a passing rain cloud, eventually the sun will come out. I guess that all of us feel at some time in our working life that we just have to hunker down—that sooner or later the storm will pass. One day the icicles of the Big Freeze will melt and we will feel more like *Glowing*.

Looking back on these times for myself and observing the lives of others, I have come to the conclusion that the "wisdom" of patience is a myth. The hard fact is that unless you act, the Big Freeze may never melt, and you may never *Glow*. I know this is a scary thought—and as I write it down, I imagine a world of constant Big Freeze with no respite. But it could happen. You could wait a long, long time for the Big Freeze to end. The important personal quality here is not patience. On the contrary, it is your capacity to act—consciously and deliberately to take the actions that will ensure that you *Glow* and find energy and innovation in your working life.

You don't have to wait to *Glow*—you can take action right now to increase the probability of Hot Spots emerging in your working life.

An Introduction to the Glow Profile

As you progress through the three principles, you and your colleagues have the opportunity to complete the *Glow* Profile for each of the principles in turn.

The concentric circles of the *Glow* Profile in Figure 2.1 are divided into three segments, representing the three principles (cooperative mindset, jumping across worlds, and igniting latent energy). The inner circle correspond to you and your work; the middle circle represents your immediate colleagues or team; and the outer circle your wider community, business, or network within which you work.

You will complete the profile as you go through each of the following chapters, starting with the segment on cooperative mindset in Chapter Three,

The *Glow* Profile

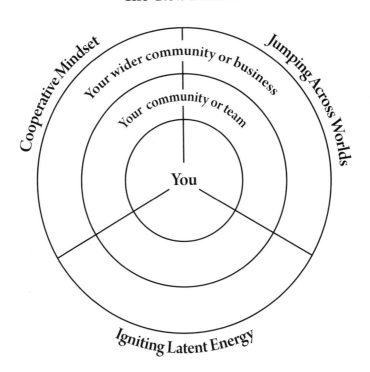

FIGURE 2.1 The *Glow* Profile

jumping across worlds in Chapter Eight, and igniting latent energy in Chapter Thirteen. For each of the three principles, you will answer a series of questions that reveal to what extent the principle is operating in your work life, in your immediate community or team, and in your wider community or business. Each of the nine segments is rated as "high" (much support for *Glowing*), "medium" (some support for *Glowing*), or "low" (limited support for *Glowing*).

By rating each of the nine segments, you can tell at a glance what aspects of your working life are currently helping you *Glow* and where you need to take immediate action. (You can download the profile and questions at http://www.hotspotsmovement.com.)

Key Points from Chapter Two

Your *Glow* Resources

The context in which you operate and work can profoundly affect your capacity to *Glow* by becoming a supportive resource or a barrier. The principles for *Glowing* are played out across three parts of your working life:

- Your own insights, talents, capabilities, habits, and choices

- Your immediate community or team—with regard to attitudes, skills, and behaviors

- Your wider community, business, or organization—with regard to the norms of the community and the routine ways of day-to-day behavior

So as you learn to increase your capacity to *Glow*, it is important that you take into consideration these three parts of your working life.

As you increase your capability to *Glow*, keep these points in mind:

- It is not about your personality—anyone who takes the nine actions can learn to *Glow*.

- What are crucial are the everyday actions you take and habits you develop.

- Forget your pet theories and instead focus on the three principles.

- Work on all three principles, rather than concentrating on the one or two that are easiest for you. The three principles are integrated, and you have to take action on all three to get the result you want.

- Find a few supportive people to engage with who can also profile themselves, and remember to listen and not become too defensive with one another.

- Patience is a myth. Take action now!

Chapter Three

The First Principle:
A Cooperative Mindset

You have said a resounding yes to staying ahead of the curve, to being able to create and flourish in high-energy places. You want a life where you *Glow*, a working life of exhilaration, energy, and insight. You have also said a resounding no to a life dominated by the Big Freeze of political intrigue and gut-churning politics.

So let's start with the first principle, developing a cooperative mindset. You will begin by completing the *Glow* Profile for cooperation and then read how three people—Jill, John, and Gareth—challenged themselves to become more cooperative and to *Glow* on a daily basis by taking action around the three cooperative actions:

Action 1 *Developing the daily habits of cooperation,* such as sharing valuable information with others, acting with discretion, using cooperative language, and making and keeping commitments

Action 2 *Mastering the art of great conversation* with both emotional authenticity and analytical rigor

Action 3 *Having the savvy to act on the "smell of the place"* by knowing the signs of the Big Freeze and moving to teams and communities where cooperation flourishes

When I asked people who *Glow* what it meant to be cooperative, this is what they said of their experiences:

"I felt completely in sync with the rest of the people."

"I felt I could trust the people I was working with."

"It was a very positive and exuberant experience for me."

"I knew that if I had any real difficulties, they were there to help me."

"I feel incredibly excited about the possibilities."

"I knew that we were all in this together, and it was a good feeling."

"It was a real pleasure to support the others in the team."

Reflect for a moment on your experience of *Glowing*. My guess is that you felt especially positive about other people.

Let's contrast this with how people described being in the Big Freeze:

"I felt consumed by rage."

"No one really trusted anyone else."

"We were always covering our backs."

"Politics and bad feelings were rife."

"We kept breaking up into smaller groups and protecting our turf."

"I got home every night exhausted from the mental strain."

"You never knew what others were saying about you."

Sound familiar? I guess all of us have at one time or another been trapped in the Big Freeze. So why is cooperation so crucial, and why is the Big Freeze so caustic?

Why You Have to Cooperate to Glow

Perhaps, like Fred, you think that to stay ahead of the curve, you need to concentrate on yourself and to work on your own. My guess is that Fred had in his mind the picture of the genius working in solitude, thinking deeply, and finally coming up with a solution that transforms the way people think or inventing a product that makes a huge contribution. He pictures this genius laboring all alone, great thoughts their only company. Finally, after years in solitary, the genius has a breakthrough, an insight, a eureka moment. Perhaps that's what Fred was trying to achieve when he closed the door and increased his working hours.

The mistake Fred made was that his image of the isolated genius is a fantasy. It does not exist in real life. In almost all known cases of people being innovative and adding true value, it was the result of working collaboratively with others. It is this mix of people full of energy and different ideas, mindsets, experiences, arguments, and conflicts that creates the context in which innovation can emerge. If you want to launch an idea or grow a business, cooperation with other people is essential. No matter how brilliant you are as a person, you cannot do it alone.

The challenge of cooperation is this: it is easy to cooperate with people whom you already know, who are similar to you, and who may even be sitting right down the corridor. That's cooperation in its simplest form; you really need just a few basic cooperation skills to interact with people you know and see often. But if you want to *Glow*, you will increasingly be with people who are different from you and who work in other locations. Cooperating with people who are virtually strangers and who are very different from you is much harder. In fact, it requires a level of goodwill and trust and a set of cooperation habits that go far beyond the basic.

To *Glow* by cooperating with others, you have to learn the skills of cooperation. I was particularly struck by this in a recent study my colleagues and I did on whether teams of people had created Hot Spots of innovation. We discovered that people who were prepared to cooperate established trust with their colleagues throughout their network. The people and teams who did not cooperate failed to become innovative and instead hoarded their knowledge, refusing to share important ideas with others. Team members saw themselves as being in competition with one another for resources. They believed they had to fight to get attention or to get access to clients or to be promoted. As you will see later in John's story, although this competition between people is sometimes taken as a sign of energy and focus, it is in fact more likely to lead to suboptimal outcomes for team members and the team as a whole.

The Glow Profile

Let's begin by taking a closer look at how cooperation is playing out in the three parts of your working life by completing the cooperative portion of the *Glow* Profile.

Profiling the First Principle: A Cooperative Mindset

The rating scales in Figure 3.1 will help you determine your own beliefs regarding cooperation, how the members of your immediate team or community work together, and how your wider community, business, or organization behaves.

Respond to each statement by circling your reaction on the 5-point scale, as follows:

5 = agree completely
4 = agree somewhat
3 = neither agree nor disagree
2 = disagree somewhat
1 = disagree completely

Once you have responded to all the statements in Figure 3.1, add up your ratings in each section; they will range from 9 to 45.

36 to 45 = high
26 to 35 = moderate
 9 to 27 = low

Now move on to the *Glow* Profile in Figure 3.2. In the "cooperative mindset" segment of the figure, use different colors or a coding scheme such as the one shown to indicate the level of cooperation in each area of your work life.

Am I naturally cooperative?

- I believe that the best way to succeed in work is through working with others.   5 4 3 2 1
- People would describe me as someone who enjoys supporting and nurturing others.   5 4 3 2 1
- People would describe me as very cooperative.   5 4 3 2 1
- I am always the first person to ask others if they need help.   5 4 3 2 1
- I always behave to others in a cooperative way.   5 4 3 2 1
- Generally, I trust other people to do the best they can.   5 4 3 2 1
- I believe that sharing my knowledge with others is important to the whole team.   5 4 3 2 1
- It is important to me that people behave in a fair manner.   5 4 3 2 1
- People say that I am good at appreciating other people.   5 4 3 2 1

Is my team naturally cooperative?

- Members of this team trust each other.   5 4 3 2 1
- Team members cover for each other.   5 4 3 2 1
- On this team, people are pleased to help each other out.   5 4 3 2 1
- On this team, the best way to get ahead is to cooperate with others.   5 4 3 2 1
- On this team, people willingly share information with one another.   5 4 3 2 1
- Around here, leaders encourage people to work cooperatively.   5 4 3 2 1
- On this team, we are able to talk openly about the conflicts that arise.   5 4 3 2 1
- We treat each other with respect.   5 4 3 2 1
- We appreciate each other's talents.   5 4 3 2 1

Is my wider community, business, or organization naturally cooperative?

- Leaders are seen to cooperate well with one another.   5 4 3 2 1
- It is the norm to coach others.   5 4 3 2 1
- We take social responsibility very seriously.   5 4 3 2 1
- We treat each other in a just and fair way.   5 4 3 2 1
- People are assessed for their cooperative work when it comes to evaluating their performance.   5 4 3 2 1
- Very competitive people do not flourish around here.   5 4 3 2 1
- We use the word *we* more than the word *I*.   5 4 3 2 1
- People are encouraged to spend time in conversation.   5 4 3 2 1
- Being able to work as part of a team is an important selection criterion.   5 4 3 2 1

FIGURE 3.1 Cooperation in the Three Areas of Your Work Life

The *Glow* Profile

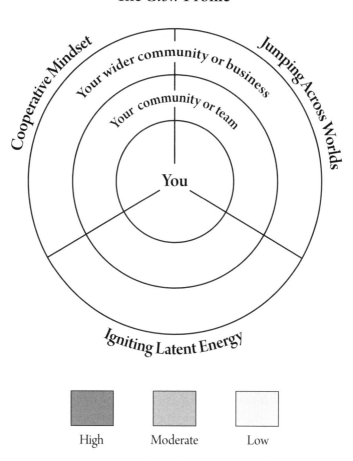

FIGURE 3.2 Your Cooperative Profile

Interpreting the Cooperative Profile

Take a look at your cooperation profile, and select the type closest to yours:

Profile Type A: Your score for cooperation is high, and so are the scores for the team and the community

You are a natural collaborator with others, you have a naturally cooperative way of looking at the world, and you have developed the skills of cooperation. Cooperation is relatively easy for you. You are in a team or community

Profile Type	Your Score	Team or Community Score	Wider Community Score
A	High	High	High
B	Moderate or High	Moderate	Moderate
C	Moderate or High	Low	Low
D	Low	Moderate or High	Moderate or High
E	Low	Low	Low

that is naturally cooperative and works on a day-to-day basis in a collaborative way. You are also in a wider community, business, or organization where there are strong cooperative norms and behaviors and the leaders behave in a cooperative way.

You are in a context in which there is a high probability of Hot Spots arising, and you are in a great frame of mind to make the best of these places and times of high energy and innovation—if the other two principles are in place.

Actions to Take   You are in a great situation and have a wonderful opportunity to *Glow* and to find and flourish in Hot Spots. Review Actions 1, 2, and 3 (Chapters Five, Six, and Seven) to ensure there is not more you could be doing. But the main action for you is to analyze the principles of jumping across worlds and igniting latent energy to make sure that the potential energy of cooperation is able to be tapped.

Profile Type B: Your score for cooperation is moderate or high, and the team and community scores are moderate

You are a natural collaborator with others, you have a naturally cooperative way of looking at the world, and you have developed the skills of cooperation. Cooperation is relatively easy for you. However, you are in a team or a wider community that does not value cooperation so highly. Working cooperatively is not a very strong capability or the natural way of working for this team. Remember, though, that the team or community does have the potential to be cooperative, and this potential can be developed by working on the habits of cooperation and learning the art of conversation.

Actions to Take   You have the great advantage of being naturally cooperative and now need to engage with others to encourage them to become more cooperative. Your first action is to engage them with these concepts: join with your colleagues as a learning group, and discuss how to become more cooperative. If your own cooperative score is moderate, you need to take a closer look at Action 1—developing the daily habits of cooperation— to strengthen your own cooperative skills. With regard to the team, work together to look at Actions 1 and 2 (Chapters Five and Six), in which you can together practice the art of great conversation.

Profile Type C: Your score for cooperation is moderate or high, and the team and community scores are low

You are a natural collaborator with others, you have a naturally cooperative way of looking at the world, and you have developed the skills of cooperation. Cooperation is relatively easy for you. However, you are a cooperative person caught in a Big Freeze. You are on a team or in a community that is competitive. People just don't trust each other enough to create a Hot Spot or to support team members to *Glow*.

Actions to Take   You can support the team by sharing these diagnostics and engaging in Action 1, developing the daily habits of cooperation, and Action 2, mastering the art of great conversation (see Chapters Five and Six). Or you can choose to work less with this team and find projects and teams that are more cooperative or a wider community or organization that is more in sync with your own values. If you decide to take this action, look carefully at Action 3—acting on the "smell of the place"—and moving to places where cooperation flourishes (see Chapter Seven). Ensure that you don't make the same mistake again by becoming more astute at spotting low-cooperation places.

Profile Type D: Your score for cooperation is low, and the team and community scores are moderate or high

Until now, you have not valued cooperation or learned the habits of cooperation. As you will see in Chapter Four, Jill was in a similar position when she began her working life. Like you, she had been brought up thinking that the best way to stay ahead of the curve was to compete with her colleagues. But when she found herself in a more cooperative situation, her behavior and attitudes began to change, and she became more cooperative.

Actions to Take   You are in a great position to build your cooperative habits because you have around you people who work cooperatively with each other. So take a closer look at Action 1, developing the daily habits of cooperation, to see how you can develop (see Chapter Five).

Profile Type E: Your score for cooperation is low, and so are the team and community scores

You are probably already feeling you are in the Big Freeze and wondering how you got there. The challenge is that it will be difficult for you to create Hot Spots of energy or innovation because you don't trust people and you are on a team or in a wider community that is also untrusting and highly competitive.

Actions to Take   This is the time to think about your options and your future. As you will see later, there is a cycle of reinforcement that creates cooperative or competitive contexts—and you are in a cycle that has created a competitive context. So you need to think carefully about Action 1, developing the daily habits of cooperation, although you may find it difficult to really gain traction if you are in the Big Freeze (see Chapter Five). You might also consider trying Action 2, mastering the art of great conversation (see Chapter Six). This may give you more of a way into conversations about how to create energy and innovation. If you want to become more cooperative, you will have to consider Action 3, acting on the "smell of the place," and become more skilled at spotting teams and communities that are cooperative (see Chapter Seven).

In Chapter Four, we'll take a closer look at how these different profiles affected the work of Jill, who moved to Profile Type A; John, who is in Profile Type D; and Gareth, a cooperative person in a very uncooperative place—Profile Type C.

Key Points in Chapter Three

The First Principle: A Cooperative Mindset

Being able to cooperate with others is crucial to you capacity to *Glow*. In this chapter, you used the *Glow* Profile to determine where you stand with regard to your own attitudes and skills, your team's attitudes and skills, and the extent to which your company or community encourages you to be cooperative. From the profile you are able to determine which cooperative profile type is nearest to your own:

Profile Type A   You, the team you work with, and your wider community are highly cooperative, which creates a marvelous opportunity for you to *Glow*.

Profile Type B   You, your team, and the wider community are skilled in some aspects of cooperation, which suggests that Action 1, developing the daily habits of cooperation, will be crucial, while learning the art of conversation in Action 2 will also be useful.

Profile Type C   You are fairly cooperative but find yourself in a Big Freeze of limited cooperation, which suggests that you need to first concentrate on building your own cooperative skills, but then think seriously about taking Action 3, acting on the "smell of the place."

Profile Type D   You are not cooperative but find yourself surrounded by a relatively cooperative team and community, which presents a terrific opportunity for you to learn from others. Think about how Action 1, developing the daily habits of cooperation could make a real difference.

Profile Type E   Neither you, your team, nor the larger community values cooperation—which gives you and your team a great opportunity to think about the effect this is having and together work on Actions 1, 2 and 3.

Chapter Four

Stories About the Warmth of Cooperation and the Big Freeze

When Cooperation Flourishes: Jill's Story

As soon as I walked into Jill's office, I could hear the buzz; it was obviously a Hot Spot of energy and excitement, and Jill was *Glowing*. I wanted to know why. This is Jill's story.

I am a very driven person. From an early age I knew what I wanted to be and have always worked really hard to get there. My passion was always for design. I love the process of thinking about something and then bringing it to fruition. For me the way I judge myself is the quality of my work—I have really high standards for myself and others and am known to push my colleagues really hard at times. When I was at design school, I was really focused on developing my own skills—I wanted to be the best designer in the college.

When I left design college, I joined a small design team. At first I loved the work, really relishing working on my own and bringing my ideas to fruition. Then I began to feel more and more uncomfortable. I found I was not sleeping very well at night and often felt a pit of anxiety in the stomach. I began to realize that one of the reasons was that people had begun to move away from me. At college we worked pretty much on our own, and I was used to doing my own thing. Here in the design studio I continued to work like this—getting in early in the morning, working on my project, and leaving late at night. I felt increasingly exhausted and isolated.

So in my late twenties I had to make a real choice about how I wanted to work. I began to realize that I was not seen as someone who could work easily with others. In fact, the rest of the team seemed to work well together, but I was excluded. I was seen as the person who worked only for herself, who liked to work on her own and to take all the credit. I realized that because I was working so hard on my own projects, I rarely noticed that others had great ideas as well and that there were occasions when my particular skills would be useful for the rest of the team.

For me the real shock came when at the end of six months' work on a project, it came time to show the work to the clients. I was really pleased with mine and thought that it was the best piece of work I had done. I had used all my skills and worked incredibly hard.... So you can imagine how shocked I was at the reception the clients gave to my work. Although I had done the very best I could, there were two areas of the design that I had completely failed to understand. I had not really come to grips with how the product I'd designed could be manufactured, and the prototype I had created was going to be too costly to mass-market. It began to dawn on me that because I had worked so hard on my own, I had not had the benefit of my colleagues' insights and knowledge of the manufacturing process and of costing feasibility.

Looking back, that client presentation was a life-changing event for me. I began to realize that if I was going to excel in the way I wanted to, I had to learn to cooperate with others in a more skillful and thoughtful way. I had to make cooperation my day-to-day habit, and I had to get better at listening to and conversing with others. I was lucky that on my team there was already a strong ethos and norms about cooperation. The team members often had lunch together, and they worked really hard to support one another. In fact, they even worked together to recruit new people to the design studio, each interviewing the person and then deciding together whether they would want to work with that person and how this potential recruit would add to the skills of the team. Once I set to work on it, I found it really easy to cooperate with others. For example, one of the practices we have is that whenever people visit our team from one of the other teams, we always try to have a brown-bag lunch for them and ask them to talk about what they are working on right now and what interests and fascinates them for the future. My team has been doing this for some time now, and I guess it is just the way that we do things around here.

I have also noticed how well the people on the senior team get on with one another. Don't get me wrong—it is not all a bed of roses, and sometimes there are some really deep disagreements. But you can see that they respect and trust each other and have the best interests of the studio at heart.

What strikes you about Jill's story? Did you hear in it echoes of Fred, who also thought that success would come from hunkering down and minimizing his relationships with colleagues? What's interesting about Jill's story is that she had great resources working with her. Both her immediate colleagues and the place that she worked supported her to become more cooperative. So if you plot Jill's cooperative profile in the three potential resources

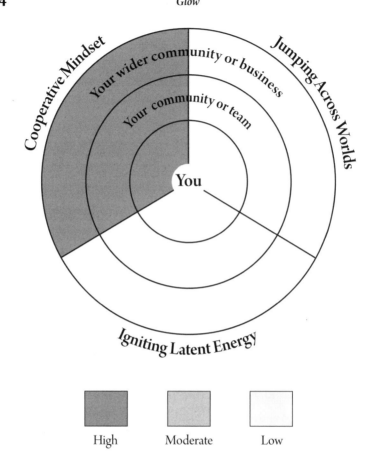

FIGURE 4.1 Jill's Cooperative Profile

(herself, her colleagues and immediate team, and her wider community or business), as Figure 4.1 shows, all three resources are helping her *Glow*.

Looking back at your own cooperative profile, how similar is it to Jill's? The interesting part of Jill's story is that she did not start out cooperative. In her initial art school training, she had been encouraged to work independently of others. When she began work, she brought this mindset with her and continued to work in an independent way, regarding others as her competition. What changed Jill was the debacle of the client presentation.

This was a real "crucible experience" for Jill and a wake-up call about how she might have to change her attitudes and skills. This experience taught

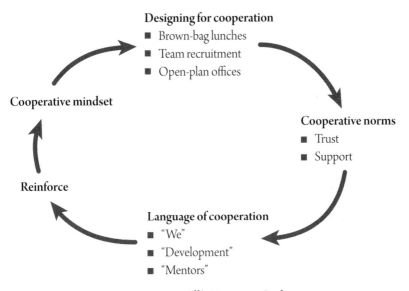

FIGURE 4.2 Jill's Virtuous Cycle

her that she was not going to be able to become what she wanted without the support of others.

This was so important to her that she vowed to develop cooperative habits. Jill had to learn to be cooperative with others, despite the fact that she had been trained to compete rather than cooperate.

What really helped Jill develop these cooperative habits was that she worked on a team that practiced cooperation. Her colleagues listened to each other; they were prepared to give each other time and on occasions worked to support each other. The third part of Jill's work life—the design company where she worked—is also very cooperative. Cooperative practices abound. People are selected on the basis of their ability to work as a team, and the brown-bag lunches provide a great informal place for conversation. At the same time, the senior team set strong cooperative role models through the way the members work with one another. In a sense, all three parts of Jill's work life are now aligned around cooperation.

What has happened to Jill is that all three potential resources (her own attitudes and skills, her team and colleagues, and the company) are working together in what has become a virtuous cycle. This virtuous cycle is shown in Figure 4.2.

Jill has joined a design agency that believes in cooperation. In a sense, the place in which she works has been designed for cooperation. This is apparent in the way in which the whole team recruits new joiners, the habit of meeting informally for brown-bag lunches, and the open plan of the office, which encourages people to meet informally. All these are subtle ways of encouraging cooperation. As Jill spends more time in the company, she begins to behave in a more cooperative way. It becomes increasingly the norm for her to trust and support others and to expect them to trust her. So the language she uses is the language of cooperation; she uses words like *we* and *colleague* and *cooperation*.

So even though Jill worked on her own for her first six months at the company, as the tasks became more complex, she needed to focus on being more cooperative. Jill has been given a wonderful opportunity to *Glow* at work and to use her cooperative mindset as the basis of creating, finding, and flourishing in Hot Spots.

Reflecting on Jill's Story

As you think about Jill's story, ask yourself three questions:

1. How would you describe your initial education and training— was it like Jill's, encouraging you to compete with others and not develop the habits of cooperation? Action 1, developing the daily habits of cooperation, can help you learn how to build cooperation even if you have not been trained for it (see Chapter Five).

2. On what basis have you decided whether to join a network, business, or community? Jill was lucky to join a cooperative community—but as we shall see in John's story, others are not as fortunate. If you want to be more sophisticated about how you choose, Action 3, acting on the "smell of the place," provides tips and questions on how to do this (see Chapter Seven).

3. Have you ever had "crucible experiences" like Jill's client meeting, when events go badly wrong? Looking back on those experiences, what can you learn from them—and is the basic problem, as in Jill's case, one of lack of trust and goodwill?

When the Big Freeze Emerges: John's Story

Although Jill started her career with a highly individual and independent mindset, over time she used all three potential resources available to her to create a work life that enabled here to *Glow*. Her profile is similar to what was identified as Profile Type A in Chapter Three. Looking back on Jill's story, her crucible experience was the client meeting, which served as the wake-up call she needed to push her to develop cooperative habits.

But what happens when the resources around you do not encourage you to cooperate and *Glow*? When you are in a place where there is very little support for cooperation? When you are in Profile Type C? This is what happened to John.

Some years ago I was invited to advise a business that seemed to have much going for it. The mission of the business was to create innovative products in financial services and to act as a boutique for a couple of industry sectors. The founders had done everything they thought they should. They had carefully and systematically recruited clever people and some real experts to run the business. However, as I worked with the business, it became clear to me that all was not going according to plan. The hoped-for innovations were not taking place, and clients complained that they were disappointed with the people they worked with. They just did not have the sparkle the clients had expected. And it was not just the clients who were disappointed. I checked the turnover of talented people and saw that it was high. In fact, over the previous year, the business had lost four of its most talented young people. I began by talking with some of the younger people on the teams and also took a closer look at how people behaved toward one another on a daily basis. As part of the interview cycle I spoke with John—and subsequently followed up with him over the next six months. This is John's story.

> I did well in college. My grades were always good, and I was seen as a great student. I loved sports and spent much of my time outside of studying on the sports field. My specialty was the track events, and at one stage I got through to the college finals. I was really proud of what I had achieved.

When I left college, I joined one of the boutique financial firms. My job was to work as an analyst, so I had to collect and analyze data from companies in a given sector. In fact, I became something of an expert in the oil and gas sector. So I was delighted when after a year I was head-hunted to work with a newly formed financial research house. I was delighted to be part of the company; I knew the reputation of a couple of the founding partners and was very pleased to be working with them.

I have now been in the firm for two years, working as a research analyst in the oil sector. We tend to work separately as analysts. There are a couple of other people also specializing in the oil and gas sector, and I guess you would say we are in competition with each other. Every six months we each write a review of what we believe will happen in the sector, and the analyst with the strongest report is given a bonus.

Ours is a competitive firm. Each of the partners came from a different company, and they launched the business on the back of their expertise. The most important way to progress in the firm is to work with one of the founders—no one else really matters. I have a strong working relationship with Celia, one of the founders who specializes in the oil and gas sector. I spend a lot of time working on her clients. Some of my colleagues are somewhat jealous of this working relationship, but I know that finding a sponsor will be key to being promoted at the firm. By working with Celia, I get to know stuff that they don't. But I am always careful to keep this knowledge to myself; I don't want to let her down.

I guess I don't feel great about working here. Sometimes the sheer competition between us gets me down. I cannot really talk with others about what they are doing because we are all in competition with each other. We use a lot of battle talk around here—winners and losers. We call our rooms "war rooms," and when we make a sale to a client, we call it "taking the big game down." It can be fun at times, but lots of people cannot take it and leave. I guess I am hoping going to get the most out of it before I move on.

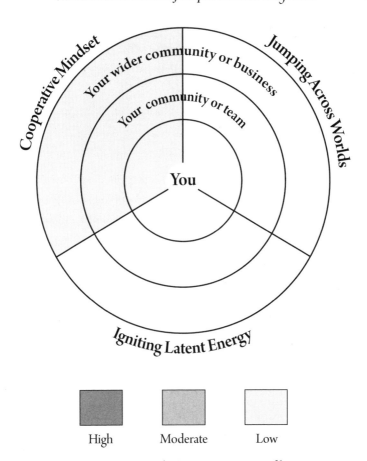

FIGURE 4.3 John's Cooperative Profile

John is not *Glowing*, and he is in a place where the Big Freeze is definitely taking its toll. How did this happen? John's personal beliefs, his team, and his wider community are not resources that are helping him *Glow*. He and his colleagues see each other in an instrumental way—"What can this person do for me?"—and in a highly competitive light—"How can I do better than the others?" His cooperative profile is shown in Figure 4.3.

John has failed to build the virtuous cycle that Jill has and that you saw in Figure 4.2. Instead he is caught in a vicious cycle that is becoming increasingly "dog eat dog." John was trained to be competitive, but unlike

Jill, he did not have a crucible experience that forced him to look inside himself. He also joined a company where competitiveness is the norm. The place is designed for competition; you can see it in the way people behave toward one another and in the ranking and bonus systems. The language is the language of competition. John and his colleagues use the word *I* more than *we*; they argue strongly from their own corner and have little trust in others. The normal way to behave is competitively—these competitive norms encourage John and his colleagues to negotiate with each other; they engage in "tit for tat" conversation and always work for their own self-interest. As self-interest rather than cooperation becomes the normal way of behaving for John, he and his colleagues come increasingly to regard knowledge as power. So they begin to hoard rather than share knowledge. The Big Freeze will begin to take over. With the Big Freeze will go any opportunities for John to work with others and combine his expertise and knowledge as Jill was able to do when she created something novel and learned to *Glow*. The cycle illustrated in Figure 4.4 gives you an idea of how the momentum of self-interest eventually leads to a Big Freeze.

On the face of it, you would imagine that John's company is a place where innovation and Hot Spots would flourish. It looks like it should be productive. John heard the words of competition, words like battlefields and wars and tournaments and winning. He saw these words as epitomizing power and energy and believed them to be harbingers of productivity and innovation. However, they turned out not to be. Instead, this is a place where knowledge is hoarded and negative competition is rife. Working in this company, John has lost his capacity to collaborate with others and has begun to lose trust in others. The competitive nature of John's company has pitted him against his colleagues, so he sees competition around each corner and begins to be a little paranoid about the world; he no longer *Glows*.

There are some of the same elements here as in Fred's story. Remember how he closed the door and vowed to work harder and harder? Like Fred, John's energy and emotional strength are beginning to be sapped by his own attitudes and his workplace. His paranoia saps his emotional energy and destroys the possibility of friendships. His emotional state also stops him from sharing his ideas with others.

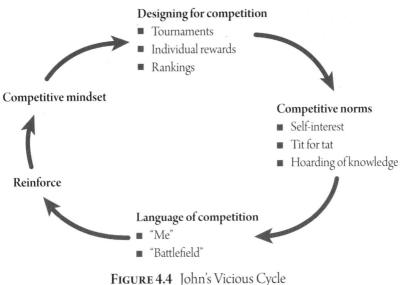

FIGURE 4.4 John's Vicious Cycle

The interesting reflection here is that while on the face of it, such gung-ho, macho environments give the impression that competition drives growth, yet in reality, they serve only to destroy the relationships, collaboration, and trust that are so crucial to Hot Spots and the possibility of anyone learning to *Glow*.

Thinking about Jill's and John's stories, what I find striking is how similar they began. Both Jill and John are the products of an education process that favors working individually. However, their paths took different routes when they left college and began to work. Jill joined a team and a company where over time she developed the habits and practices of cooperation. John's career took a different path. In his company, he expected to work individually and competitively with his colleagues. His performance was pitted against others, and so he failed to develop the habits of cooperation.

Reflecting on John's Story

As you think about John's story, ask yourself three questions:

1. What is your basic attitude about how you are going to be successful? Take a look at your competitive profile and see how you scored.

Are you like John in believing that your success will come through competing with others?

2. How do your colleagues on your immediate team behave toward one another? Are they, like Jill's colleagues, likely to be potential resources for you? Or are they like John's colleagues, likely to work against you? Remember that in a highly competitive world, everyone is competing with each other to *Glow*. In a cooperative world, everyone is helping each other *Glow*.

3. If you are surrounded by highly competitive people, where can you start? One thought is to look at Action 1, developing the daily habits of cooperation, to identify how you can make the first move to change the nature of the place (see Chapter Five). Also take a look at Action 2, mastering the art of great conversation, to consider how you might begin the conversation (see Chapter Six).

Jill's cooperative profile is aligned around cooperation, while John's is aligned around competition. What happens when you find that you want to be cooperative but are surrounded by competitive people? That's what Gareth found.

When a Cooperative Person Ends Up in a Big Freeze: Gareth's Story

As soon as you meet Gareth, you know he is one of life's naturally cooperative people. Well-spoken, he handles himself with grace and ease. His voice rarely rises in tempo, and he has a reputation for fairness. This is his story.

Even as a child, I was concerned about others. My parents still remark on how I used to talk to the old lady who lived next door and occasionally take small gifts to her. I always saw myself in relation to others. It was important to me to think of the needs of others. As I grew up, this value and way of being stayed with me. I have no idea really where this attitude came from—perhaps I was very influenced by an uncle whom people say I am very much like.

When I completed college, I went to join one of the large companies—you would know its brand names. I had joined as a graduate trainee and really enjoyed my three years there. I was part of a whole gang of graduates who joined at the same time. We really supported each other, helped each other out, and generally looked out for each other. Within a couple of years, the CEO asked a group of us to be a "shadow board" and to come up with suggestions about the future direction of the products. These were some of the most exciting times of my working life—true Hot Spots! I was working with people from across the world, in a really cooperative and trusting way, on a task that we all found tough but challenging. By the end of the project, we reported to the CEO and basically talked to him about the real challenges we faced bringing sustainability into the design, production, and distribution of the products. Looking back, I can see that we began to understand the green issues before many others had. Well, we were young and in this hypercreative frame of mind.

The work we all did was considered really crucial. The CEO referred to the team in one of his major speeches and began to assemble a number of project teams around the areas we had identified. Many of us stayed on to work on one of the project teams.

After another year, I decided to leave. The time was right; I felt I wanted to broaden my experience and move to another sector. So I applied to and received an offer from another company. I was delighted. It meant a bigger salary, more power and decision making, and a greater capacity to influence the longer-term strategy of the business.

The first month or two were just what I had expected. It was a great job, and I had the power to make decisions and really forge ahead. By that time I was married and had two small children. It was after about six months that my wife mentioned to me that my mood had seemed to change. She caught me being bad-tempered with the children, and I was always on a short fuse. At the same time, I began to feel uneasy at work. I had worked the way I always had since I was a child. I thought hard about the issues, engaged my colleagues in conversations about possible solutions, and then shared these with the leaders of the business.

Yet there had been a couple of times when I realized that my colleagues were not giving me the whole story—they were holding information back. Occasionally this was really important to the success of the project. In fact, there had been a very memorable occasion when I had been presenting to the business leaders and realized that I had severely underestimated the cost of one of the areas we were working in. At the time I felt stupid—but looking back and analyzing the situation, I realized that one of my colleagues had deliberately withheld the information from me because he wanted the promotion I was in line for.

Over the next six months, it became worse. I simply reverted to the cooperative behavior I had known best, but I began to realize that while I was sharing important and useful information and supporting others, this was rarely reciprocated. I realized that this was a race and I seemed to be losing. When one of my less competent colleagues was promoted ahead of me, that was the last straw. My wife and I talked it over, and I decided to leave the company and try to find a place that was more resonant with my own values.

Gareth's cooperative profile is shown in Figure 4.5. As you can see, Gareth is a cooperative person who found himself in a highly competitive place where he was not succeeding and certainly not *Glowing*. In fact, it sounds as if he ended up in the Big Freeze, the sort of dog-eat-dog place John also found himself in.

Gareth made one big mistake: he left his old team and company to join another business without understanding what he was getting himself into. As a result, he ended up working in a highly competitive place where he was exploited for his good nature.

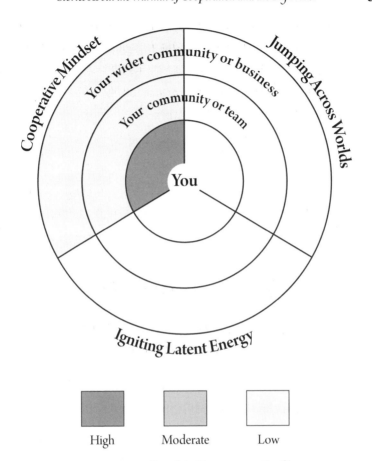

FIGURE 4.5 Gareth's Cooperative Profile

Reflecting on Gareth's Story

As you think about Gareth's story, ask yourself three questions:

1. Think back to your first job. Did it encourage you to be cooperative, or were you encouraged to compete with others?

2. Have you ever found yourself on a team or in a community or business where you felt out of sync with everyone else? Like Gareth, have you ever tried to cooperate and simply ended up feeling exploited? If that's the case, you need to become much savvier about

the teams and places you are thinking of joining before you join. As Gareth found, having these insights after you have joined is too late. If you are in such a situation, take a close look at Action 3 to see how you can avoid making the same mistake again and be savvier about where you join (see Chapter Seven).

3. Have you had crucible experiences that really shook you up? If so, how have you used these experiences to help you grow and *Glow*?

Now is the time to reflect on your cooperation profile and to consider which of the three actions discussed in Chapters Five, Six, and Seven are going to be most crucial to you.

Key Points in Chapter Four

Stories About the Warmth of Cooperation and the Big Freeze

In these stories, we learned about three people and their experiences of cooperation. The key lessons from these stories are as follows:

- Some people, like Gareth, have learned to be cooperative from an early stage of their life, while others, like John, have been brought up to be competitive. These basic attitudes can be a resource that helps you *Glow* or an impediment that plunges you into the Big Freeze.

- However, even people like Jill who have been trained to be highly individualistic and competitive can learn new habits and skills. In Action 1, developing the daily habits of cooperation, you will see what Jill did to become more cooperative (see Chapter Five).

- Immediate colleagues and community are crucial resources in learning new habits and skills. In Jill's case, her immediate colleagues created a virtuous cycle in which the way they worked together, the language they used, and the norms of their behavior all created an atmosphere that encouraged Jill to be innovative, successful, and *Glow*.

■ Your colleagues can also be a real block to *Glowing*. You saw this clearly in John's story, when he foolishly joined a highly competitive team. That pitched him into a vicious cycle and made it more and more difficult to be energized, innovative, and successful. In Action 3, acting on the "smell of the place," you will learn what John should have done before he joined and thereby avoided his error (see Chapter Seven).

Chapter Five

ACTION 1

Developing the Daily Habits of Cooperation

People who Glow have positive ways of thinking about others and five daily habits of cooperation. They have realistic and positive expectations of others and are prepared to share valuable information with others, to act with discretion, to use the language of cooperation, and to make and keep commitments.

For some people, being cooperative is as easy as falling off a log. That's the case with Gareth, who has been cooperative since he was a child. Ask him what he does to be cooperative, and he will look at you in amazement—it's invisible to him; he doesn't know any other way. For other people, being cooperative does not come so naturally. They can choose not to change—and like Gareth suffer the consequences of the Big Freeze, or they can, like Jill, learn to *Glow* by actively developing the habits of cooperation.

Everyone can learn to be cooperative—it's simply a matter of will and choice and of learning a number of habits that you will depend on every day. And if you have children, these are habits you may want them to learn as well. As Jill found, it could make their working life more energized and fun.

The Nature of Habits

What are habits? Habits are actions you regularly take that become part of who you are and define the person you have become. Adopting some of these habits requires you to develop a skill or an aptitude, while others do not.

Think about a couple of habits you have developed in your working life. How have they defined who you are? What role if any have they played in your success?

As I think about these questions, I am reflecting on my own daily habits. Take today, for example. Today is a writing day for me, and I am in my home in Spain looking over the Mediterranean. Since I had planned to write today, I got up relatively early this morning to see the sunrise. Then I put on some music that I always listen to, and then my habit is to spend about ten minutes in basic yoga. I then switch to another album and go to my sofa, where I write for the next four or five hours. These habits are important to me; they define who I am (I am a writer and a researcher), and they have been crucial to my success (they enable me to be productive). By the way, as I edit this section, I am under pressure, sitting uncomfortably in an airport—sadly, being near the Mediterranean is only a small part of my life! But the habits I have developed in that place have been an important part of my productivity and my capacity to *Glow*.

Where did these habits come from? Reflecting on my own habits, five of which I just described, I see that they have been assembled over time from bits and pieces in the same way that a bird assembles a nest. I have discovered them in all sorts of places. Some I have experimented with for years. The choice of music, for example—when I am doing yoga, I always listen to something soothing but lively; at the moment, it's Jack Johnson's album *In Between Dreams* (it has the right upbeat tempo for yoga). However, I have discovered that when I am writing, I cannot listen to voices; I only listen to orchestral pieces and preferably the piano. In fact, my habit is to listen to Glenn Gould playing Bach (*The Goldberg Variations, The French Suites,* and the *Partita*). These listening habits have taken years of experimentation to develop, but they are a habit that suits me well.

The habit of lounging on the sofa when writing? Like most writers, I began to write at a desk (in fact, in my home in London, I still do write at a desk) but found that often my back and upper shoulders ached. Then I saw my great friend Tammy Erickson writing at her home in Boston lounging on a comfortable "lazy boy" chair. I liked the idea so much that I began to do the same when writing in Spain—and it has been a habit ever since.

The habits I have described are not cooperative habits; I simply use them to illustrate what habits are and how they are developed over years from a variety of experiences until they become incorporated into our everyday actions.

These are habits that have served me well, but I also have habits that have not served me so well. My habit, for example, of always wanting to have the last word. I am a determined person, and I find it really hard to let go—so I continue to push for my own view. Imagine what our household is like with teenage boys who also want to have the last word! Wanting to have the last word is not great for cooperation, and over the years I have tried to modify this habit and learn to let go, with mixed results, I would have to say.

Take time to think about some of your habits—particularly your habits around others. Where do you think these habits have come from? Are they serving you well? If the answer is no, take a closer look at the five cooperative habits discussed in this chapter and how they might replace some of your bad habits.

I have discovered that people who often seem to be in the Big Freeze have five bad habits:

- They try to keep all the good ideas and information to themselves.

- They use confidential information as a source of gossip to devalue others.

- They only talk about the really positive aspects of themselves and work hard to create an impenetrable shell.

- They use the language of combat a great deal at work—words like battle, survivors, victory, and losers.

- They are vague about what they promise and try to form a smoke screen around what they will deliver.

Now take a look at the five good habits, which at first glance seem rather simple but can be incredibly powerful.

The Five Good Cooperative Habits

If you want to *Glow*, you need to build into your daily behavior a set of habits that will enable you to cooperate with others with ease. Here are five daily habits that are crucial to developing this aspect of yourself:

- The habit of sharing valuable information with others
- The habit of acting with discretion
- The habit of being open about yourself
- The habit of using the language of cooperation
- The habit of making and keeping commitments

So lets recap: habits are the daily routines that define who you are. You have assembled these habits over time through experimentation and seeing other people behaving in those ways. Recall how Jill learned the habits of cooperation by watching the people she worked with and studying their behavior. As Jill found, where you spend your time and whom you work with can be crucial for providing role models for developing good cooperative habits.

Habits can also be manifestations of your personality and preferred style of working. For example, I am an introvert who enjoys my own company, and so the solitary habits I have accumulated while writing are a perfect manifestation of my personality and preferences.

People like Gareth, who are naturally cooperative, and people like Jill, who have learned to be cooperative, are all defined by the habits they have developed around other people. Cooperation is a habit—it is something you can learn from others and can improve with practice. You have the free will to develop these habits of cooperation if you choose to do so.

Let's take a look at each of these habits in more detail.

The Habit of Sharing Valuable Information with Others

One of the most powerful habits of cooperation you can develop is "gifting": willingly sharing valuable information with other people. Recall how Gareth began to realize that his colleagues did not have this habit or how surprised Jill was to find herself in a place where people willingly shared knowledge with her.

At the heart of your ability to be cooperative is your willingness to give without anticipating that you will receive anything in return. Your relationships with work colleagues should not take the form of transactions—you do something for them, and then they do something for you. That's what you might call tit-for-tat bartering whereby each of you is trying to maximize your own self-interest. Tit-for-tat behavior eliminates the possibility of cooperating through sharing.

Actions to take now to share valuable information with others

Action 1.1 *Identifying your possible sources of value.* First work out what you have that is valuable and could be important to others. Here are some suggestions:

- Your time or your capacity to listen to others, giving them your undivided attention

- Your network and the connections that you have developed, if connecting two people you know could be fruitful

- The ideas you have that could be beneficial to others

- Your goodwill and capacity to feel positive and upbeat about others, to wish the very best for them

Action 1.2   *Sharing these valuable resources.* Now think about what is valuable to you, consider how you might share this with others, and set yourself this task:

- Over the next week, I will willingly give something that is valuable to me to two of my nearest colleagues.

- I will not monitor what they do with my gift but will give again the following week.

The Habit of Acting with Discretion

If you want to be cooperative, you have to learn to trust people and they have to learn to trust you. When you trust others, you take their goodwill for granted and don't need to keep checking the motives for their actions. When you are perceived as a trustworthy person, this encourages cooperation in your wider circle because trust permits easy relationships with people who don't yet know each other well. One of the ways that you demonstrate you are trustworthy is the way you handle sensitive information. People are more likely to trust you if they see you acting with discretion.

Actions to take now to act with discretion

Action 1.3   *Acting with discretion.* Ask yourself the following questions:

- What confidential information have you been entrusted with? This could be information about people, or the organization or community that you are a member of.

- Looking back over the last couple of months are there times when you have been indiscreet? Times when you have told people information that was given to you in confidence, or occasions when you gave away information that you knew to be sensitive and should not have been shared?

- As you reflect on your actions over the last couple of months, remind yourself that sharing confidential information will seriously erode your ability to be seen as being discreet and trustworthy.

The Habit of Being Open About Yourself

Cooperation flourishes when you have great conversations. As you will see in Chapter Six, conversation can be analytical (when you talk about business results, financial numbers, or trends) or emotional (when you talk about how you feel about something, what your views are, what it means to you). It is the combination of the analytical and the emotional that generates great conversations that allow you to *Glow* and fuel Hot Spots. For these great conversations to take place, you need to be open about your emotions and prepared to trust others and develop this trust in an open and authentic way.

☼ *Actions to take now to self-disclose wisely*

Action 1.4   *Deepening your self-awareness.* What is it about yourself that you feel good about, and what aspects of yourself are you trying to improve? What aspects of your colleagues do you value, and what aspects of your colleagues do you feel are working against you?

Action 1.5   *Opening up to others.* You create stronger trusting relationships by being open about what you value about yourself and what you value in others. This demonstrates goodwill toward others.

Develop trust by being open about yourself and what you are striving to change. Tell your colleagues about what you are trying to change and ask them to support you.

Be prepared to share your feelings and emotions with others in a way that is appropriate to the situation but demonstrates that you are being open with them.

The Habit of Using the Language of Cooperation

Recall that in the three stories you explored in Chapter Four, language played a key role in the development of Jill's virtuous cycle and Gareth's vicious cycle. When Gareth joined a company that was highly individually competitive, he very quickly became aware of the language of competition—always using the word *I*, for example, rather than *we*. When Jill joined a more cooperative place, she began to trust and cooperative with people because she heard more cooperative language.

☼ *Actions to take now to develop the language of cooperation*

Action 1.6   *Monitoring the language of cooperation.* Over the next week, monitor your use of cooperative and competitive language. You create stronger cooperation by making sure you use the word *we* rather than *I* when discussing business matters and by consciously using language that includes others to encourage *cooperation* among your *team* of *colleagues*.

The Habit of Making and Keeping Commitments

When you share valuable information with others, act with discretion, and use the language of cooperation, you are practicing habits of cooperation on a daily basis. However, there is one more habit that is essential to *Glowing*. That is the way you engage with others in the tasks and joint actions you take. Many of the Hot Spots of creativity and innovation you find yourself in will require you to work on complex tasks. Think back to how Frank went about solving the problem he faced by reaching out to the people around him. However, for this reaching out to work, Frank has to be willing to make commitments with respect to what he is prepared to do, when he is prepared to do it by, and what would be the consequences of his failing to honor these commitments. For people to trust Frank, they have to see him delivering on these promises and to be regarded as a person who is able to keep to his commitments.

Commitments lubricate the everyday practice of cooperation. By making a commitment, you agree to a course of action you will take. Without commitments, cooperation simply becomes mere window dressing—a charade that you are playing.

☼ *Actions to take now to make and keep commitments*

Action 1.7   *Making commitments.* Be prepared to make powerful commitments to people, stating clearly what you are committing to. Do this face to face or on the telephone or in a videoconference so that everyone can hear your tone of voice and can acknowledge the commitments you have made:

- State precisely what you are going to do, and declare up front the consequences you are prepared to accept if you do not live up to your promises.

- Be wise and realistic about what you can achieve and the promises you make to ensure that you are in a position to fulfill others' expectations of you. A well-intentioned tendency to overcommit and overpromise will erode the trust others have in you and their willingness to cooperate with you.

Supporting the Habit of Cooperation

As you look back on these five habits you may be asking yourself if there is more you can do to support their development. Of course these habits come from within—they are about you. However, there are ways in which you can increase their potency. Think back to Gareth, who learned the habits of cooperation from a dearly loved uncle, or how Jill learned the habits of cooperation by watching the people in her firm. The place where John worked did the opposite. The executives he worked with behaved in a highly individualistic and competitive way—and so he learned competitive habits from them.

Since you develop habits by watching others, you need to be thoughtful about whom you have around you. Spend too much time with highly competitive people, and like John, you will abandon your cooperative habits. The people who become your role models and mentors can have a profound impact on how your habits develop, so choose carefully. In fact, my own research on cooperative workplaces shows that the most important influence on the cooperative habits of individuals or teams is how they see other (often senior) people behaving. When people mentor you, they take a personal interest in you, they support your development, and it is often from them you learn your habits.

So choose your mentors with great care. This will mean at times steering clear of the person who looks most successful and instead choosing a mentor for his or her cooperative capabilities. For example, when John worked closely with Celia, the relationship between them was not particularly positive for John. Over the longer term, Celia will damage John by teaching him bad habits, such as becoming adept at tit-for-tat negotiations and never giving anything away unless he's going to get something in return. These bad habits will severely limit his pleasure at work and his capacity to *Glow*. Perhaps most damaging, a highly competitive mentor like Celia may strive to control the access her mentees have to other people. So, for example, Celia did not introduce John to any of her colleagues who had clients beyond the gas sector. A transactional relationship like this rarely helps you *Glow* because the other person is only in it for what he or she can get out of it—not what everyone can put in and gain together.

As you reflect on the five cooperative habits, think about who could be a cooperative mentor for you and take the initiative to approach them to coach you on a project you are working on. You will be surprised at how delighted they will be to coach you—after all, this is a cooperative habit.

Key Points in Chapter Five

ACTION 1
Developing the Daily Habits of Cooperation

Habits are actions you regularly take that become part of who you are and define the person you have become. The development of some habits requires you to develop skill or aptitude, while others do not. If you want to *Glow,* you need to build into your daily behavior a set of habits that will enable you to cooperate with others with ease. There are five daily habits that are crucial to developing this aspect of yourself:

The Habit of Sharing Valuable Information with Others
Cooperative people make a habit of sharing what is valuable to them with others.

Action 1.1   Identifying your possible sources of value

Action 1.2   Sharing these valuable resources

The Habit of Acting with Discretion
Cooperative people are trusted because they are discreet.

Action 1.3   Acting with discretion

The Habit of Being Open About Yourself
Cooperative people are trusted by others because they are able to be open about themselves and authentic in their behavior.

Action 1.4   Deepening your self-awareness

Action 1.5   Opening up to others

The Habit of Using the Language of Cooperation
Cooperative people demonstrate that they value cooperation by using the language of cooperation.

Action 1.6   Monitoring the language of cooperation

The Habit of Making and Keeping Commitments
Cooperative people are trusted by others because they are able to make and keep commitments.

Action 1.7   Making commitments
Remember that cooperative role models can be enormously important in supporting your cooperative habits.

Chapter Six

ACTION 2

Mastering the Art of Great Conversation

People who Glow know the art of great conversation and use conversation as the bedrock of their cooperation with others. They are able to bring emotional authenticity and analytical rigor to their conversations.

When you *Glow,* one thing that is striking is the way you talk with other people. Sure, some of your conversations will be of little consequence, but many will be considerably livelier: thought-provoking, fascinating, and purposeful. People who *Glow* and the Hot Spots they inhabit bubble with great conversation—and great conversation is what ties you together as you cooperate with others. So if you want to *Glow* by finding, flourishing, or creating Hot Spots, you'd better take a look at how you converse with others.

A Great Conversation

Here are some snippets from a high-quality conversation. We join the team of a company that markets coffee and tea; it's the very beginning of a Hot Spot that will develop as time goes on, and Adam and his colleague Barbara are beginning to cooperate with each other and share the knowledge that will enable them both to *Glow*. We drop in as they are talking about going to work on their coffee products.

> ADAM *What's really important to bringing this product to a wider market?*
>
> BARBARA *Yes, that's a question that has been on my mind as well.*
>
> ADAM *We should certainly take into consideration the latest research findings from the product launch. We found that 20 percent of consumers bought the product on the basis of a recommendation from a friend.*
>
> BARBARA *Yes, and when we ran focus groups earlier this year, we discovered that what the friends often talked about in these recommendations was the sustainability element. They really appreciate our efforts to source the ingredients from coffee suppliers at fair prices and where we have supported the coffee-growing communities.*
>
> ADAM *So in thinking about the question "How do we bring this product to a wider market?" this has to be a key consideration.*

Adam and Barbara continue to talk about this as they stroll down the corridor. Their conversation is rigorous in the sense that they brought in analytical information from the market research and focus groups. However, great conversation is not just about the ideas and knowledge, or what we might call "analytical rationality." In great conversation, you are also able to bring something of yourself—you are able to disclose your beliefs and views in a way that is authentic to who you are. This links back to the cooperation habit of being open about yourself to others. As you listen to Barbara and Adam's conversation, you can hear how it moves into the realm of emotional authenticity. We rejoin them later that day:

> BARBARA *Working with the coffee-growing communities is really important to me. It's why I joined this company in the first place. I remember when I was in college, I went to Brazil on my first break. While I was there I saw some of the really important and groundbreaking work being done in the coffee trade. I also saw what a tough deal some of the coffee growers got. I*

really valued the time I spent in Brazil and realized that this was going to be important to what I would work on and what I valued after I left college.

ADAM *Working with the communities is not so important to me. I know it makes sense to the suppliers, but personally, I am dubious of the whole thing. I wonder if it is just PR whitewash. I guess I am just a more cynical person than you are.*

BARBARA *I can understand your cynicism—but if you can give me an hour of your time next week, I would love to introduce you to a friend of mine named Ramona who has just come back from Brazil. She has been working with a group who are supporting the concept of Fair Trade from the point of growing right through to selling. I think you will find her story really compelling.*

Here you can feel the conversation moving toward the emotional as they both disclose something about how they feel. Barbara is practicing the cooperative habit of being open, and she is also sharing a valuable connection with Adam since she has decided to introduce Adam to Ramona, who is an important contact for her. Notice that Barbara is also practicing the cooperative habit of using the language of cooperation, using the word *we* and engaging Adam in her conversation. Adam is also being open when he reveals his cynicism about some of the aspects of Fair Trade. This is a high-quality conversation in that they are both sharing important analytical information and at the same time being open about their own values and experiences—so it has an element of both analytical rationality and emotional authenticity. I have discovered that people *Glow* when they are engaged in great conversations, and this creative sort of dialogue can be crucial to creating and flourishing in Hot Spots.

You will see this in Figure 6.1. The combination of analytical rationality and emotional authenticity creates four distinct types of conversations you might have. This framework can help you diagnose your own conversations, both to help you understand the causes of poor conversations and to suggest ways to achieve more creative dialogues.

Four Ways to Have a Conversation

Figure 6.1 shows that there are four ways to have a conversation. Ask yourself this question: In what way do I most typically converse, and what would it take to make my conversations more rigorous and authentic?

Dehydrated Talk

How many of your conversations are "dehydrated" and ritualized? In these conversations, you bring neither the sharpness of analytical rigor nor the warmth of emotional authenticity. These conversations contain no doubt, no curiosity, and no puzzling. Perhaps they feel to you like simply a string of trivial and unrelated fragments, which are ritualistic rather than authentic. Dehydrated talk is not the foundation for cooperation, and it certainly won't help you *Glow*. So why do you engage in it?

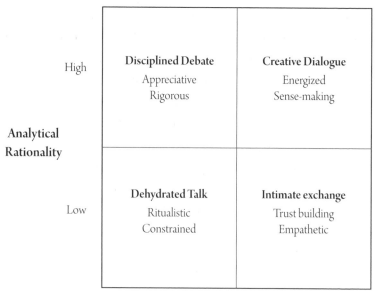

FIGURE 6.1 A Conversation Matrix.

Here is an example of what I would categorize as dehydrated talk between Barbara and her team leader, Karen, later that day.

KAREN *So how would you rate your performance this year on a one to five scale against these five competencies: innovative potential, leading others, listening and putting your view forward, project planning, and creating a vision.*

BARBARA *Well, I guess I would give myself a four on all of these—I think I have had a pretty good year, all things considered.*

KAREN *Thanks, Barbara. I will put you down as a four for all of these. Good to see you! Let's meet again soon.*

This is dehydrated talk in the sense that it contains no real facts and neither Karen nor Barbara is being particularly authentic or revealing about herself. Think about the times when dehydrated talk happens to you. My guess is that it happens most often when you are in a formalized situation, simply going through the motions. Barbara is merely going through the ritual of a performance-management conversation with her team leader. Of course, sometimes performance-management conversations can be full of feedback and insight—but more often they are simply formalized exchanges in which the outcomes were predictable.

Some dehydrated conversations are like this, well-rehearsed "set pieces" with predetermined scripts and outcomes. Other conversations become dehydrated when the agendas are tightly defined and the opportunities for exploration or discovery are constrained. Or perhaps the timing is so tight that there is no opportunity for pause or reflection. Dehydrated talk does little to help you to cooperate with others or encourage you to *Glow*, since it does not add any value to anyone.

Disciplined Debate

There are good conversations, like Barbara and Adam's initial conversation, in which analytical rigor is strong. In the conversation between Adam and Barbara, what you heard was disciplined debate. They listened to each other, appreciated each other's point of view, and brought in new information to help them address the question that Adam posed.

As you try to perfect the art of conversation, you may want to think about one of the greatest conversationalists of all times, the ancient philosopher Socrates. The so-called Socratic approach was central to Socrates's conversational style. Socrates asked carefully constructed questions, on the assumption that he could learn most from others and could contribute most to others through disciplined debate. Socrates used the art of conversation to analyze issues and ideas in a systematic way. This was his gift to others and the way in which he cooperated in debates with others.

In a disciplined debate, what you are talking about is based on fact rather than lazy thinking or prejudice. Disciplined debate can be a crucial igniter of a Hot Spot because it creates a context in which people feel prepared and able to ask the "big questions" that can engage and excite others and act as a focus for latent energy to emerge.

So how can you ensure that at least some of your conversations with others are disciplined debate? Here are two ways to think about it:

Ask vigorous and disciplined questions. These types of conversations need a Socrates—a source of vigorous and disciplined questioning. If you want to add value in your cooperation with others, you may want to ask yourself whether you are being sufficiently rigorous and analytical. In Action 7, asking questions that spark energy, you will find some ideas about how to get started (see Chapter Fourteen).

☼ Actions to take now to ask rigorous and disciplined questions

Action 2.1 *Asking rigorous and disciplined questions.* Over the course of a few days, make a note of the questions at work that strike you as interesting and important. Don't be worried if some of the questions you note down seem less than major—as Socrates found, sometimes it is in simplicity that the greatest insights can be found. When you have your list, select the two questions that seem really exciting and interesting to you at the moment, and find someone to talk with about them.

Seek high-quality and relevant information. To have a disciplined debate, you need to have high-quality and relevant information to bring to the conversation. In the disciplined debate earlier, both Adam and Barbara are bringing in new information and insights that take the debate forward. If they simply used the same information they used in the past, they would simply be repeating the same conversation. You have to get different information if you want different conversations.

☀ *Actions to take now to find high-quality and relevant information*

Action 2.2 *Finding high-quality information.* Ask yourself, "Where do I normally get my information from? Is this a narrow range? And if it is, how might I widen it?"

Remember that sometimes the most interesting and relevant information is outside your immediate circle of colleagues.

Take action to spread your information search beyond the immediate group. Take a look at Action 5, jumping out of the boundaries that constrain you, to learn ways to widen your information search (see Chapter Eleven).

Intimate Exchange

In the second conversation between Barbara and Adam, emotional empathy was high because both were prepared to share something about themselves. Barbara talked about her experience in Brazil and was open about the impact it had on her joining the company. She must have had some sense of trust in Adam to be prepared to share what could be rather private information. Adam, for his part, listened to what Barbara said and responded authentically, expressing his own feelings about the topic. Such intimate exchanges can really make a difference to the quality of conversation and ultimately to your ability to *Glow*.

One of the mistakes of the workplace, it seems to me, is to deny the role of emotions. Hot Spots arise and you *Glow* when you have an opportunity to talk about your emotions in an authentic way, to share what is exciting to you, and to connect your feelings with others. That's why the cooperative habit of being open is so important. It is during these times of authenticity that trust flourishes and cooperation is built. Yet how many times have you heard "You're being emotional" as a stern put-down when you express your feelings in the course of a conversation—the term *emotional* perhaps being used as a euphemism for *irrational.*

Emotional conversations flourish in your private life as you build trusting relationships with family and friends. You are able to talk about your emotions, explain your feelings to others, and try to understand where they are coming from. This creates the basis for appreciating others. If you are to create cooperation as a foundation for *Glowing* in your work life, you need the same level of empathy, mutual understanding, and trust at work.

Here are some actions you can take now to ensure that your conversations have the element of emotional authenticity that is so crucial to creating cooperation.

Actions to take now to be open about your emotions

Action 2.3 *Devote time to conversations.* It seems to me that one of the most pressing challenges many of us face at work is the challenge of time. Do you share my feeling that too often your conversations with others occur in snippets? Think about the last time you sat down with a colleague and gave each other undivided attention? This may well be a rare occurrence. If you want to bring emotional authenticity to your conversations and to build strong cooperative relationships with others, you have to be prepared to investment time.

Be open about your emotions, and have personal conversations. Conversations build trust and cooperation when you are being open. Think back to Barbara. By being open about her values and her experience, Barbara helped Adam know more about her. By taking the lead in opening up, she also gave Adam permission to open up about himself, even if he disagreed with her.

It can be tough to have far-ranging personal conversations, particularly if you are working in a bureaucracy where one of the essential features is depersonalization—you are expected to play defined roles, and everything that is personal about you is expected to be left at home. So the first requirement for having emotional conversations is to repersonalize the workplace; to recognize that you and your colleagues are real people, with feelings and emotions that affect your work.

Action 2.4   *Having wide-ranging conversations.* People need to know who you are and what you believe in if they are to establish a trusting relationship with you. So when you have your one-hour conversations, talk about what is important to you. You may want to begin by talking about your past experiences and your hobbies. As you become closer, you can deepen the emotional part of the conversation by talking of your family or your personal hopes for the future; your fears and apprehensions; the way you like to work; your philosophy of leadership. It is in such wide-ranging conversations that trust is built.

Action 2.5   *Asking emotional questions.* One way to get started is to do what people skilled in this do: take the lead by asking an emotion-laden question, such as "How do we feel about one another, and how could we work better together?"

Creative Dialogue

Rationality brings structure to conversations; emotions bring meaning. Rationality is deductive, focusing attention on tangible data and their interrelationships. Emotions, by contrast, are holistic, emotions deal with your feelings and ideas. As a result, the two are always hard to combine. Yet like the yin and yang of Chinese philosophy, the most creative, insightful, and energizing conversations you can have will occur when the two are combined: one hard, the other soft; one rooted in the categories of structure, the other in the images of meaning. Bringing thinking and feeling together is difficult, but if you can do it, you move from fragmentation to unity.

When you have creative dialogue, the results can be spectacular and will play a crucial role in you capacity to *Glow* and to find and flourish in high-energy Hot Spots.

Let's return to Barbara and Adam for a moment to see how their conversation became a creative dialogue. Barbara has introduced Adam to her friend Ramona, who has just returned from working with an NGO in Brazil.

RAMONA *For the last four years I have worked with the coffee growers on a small plantation in central Brazil. We are absolutely committed to supporting the growers by buying the coffee at a fair price and encouraging the communities to flourish. Let me show you some of the ways that we ensure that from the planting of the trees to the growing of the beans and then the harvesting and selling of the beans, we make sure the whole process follows Fair Trade principles. (Ramona shows Adam and Barbara a video she made on the plantation.) The video shows how farmers have used the Fair Trade income to invest in local schools, sink wells in the villages, and provide basic medical care.*

ADAM *That's pretty impressive, Ramona, but to be honest, I wonder how much the Fair Trade label really separates us from our competitors in the market.*

BARBARA *I have been wondering about that as well. When I looked more closely at the focus group data we collected, what really struck me was how much people are interested in organic coffee. I wonder if that is something we should be thinking about.*

RAMONA *That's interesting. You know, we have a growing number of plantations that are working toward organic registration. The process of registration is not easy for these farmers; it can take many years, and in the interim, life can be very tough for them. In fact, the NGO I am working with has found it hard to convince some of these farmers to continue—they see it as a more expensive way of farming and cannot see that it will bring real benefits. So until now we have had to subsidize them during the transition period to being organically certified. But that's expensive for us, and of course we can't subsidize everyone we would like to.*

ADAM *I wonder if there is something we can do to support you. Perhaps we can provide some support ourselves for these projects. We also have a whole plan for social responsibility that we could bring in. Many of our employees are really interested in supporting the communities in which we work. We should talk more about twinning our manufacturing plants with communities in Brazil. The first action is that we need to show that video to more people. Would you be willing to present it at our management conference next week? It seems to me that the combination of Fair Trade and organic coffee could be a real winner.*

In a very short space of time Ramona, Adam, and Barbara are engaged in a creative dialogue. Ramona has brought in ideas they had not considered earlier, they have all contributed to the conversation, and they have arrived at a set of possibilities that is exciting and has real potential. In other words, they are on their way to creating a Hot Spot, and by radiating energy and excitement, they are experiencing the positive emotions of *Glowing*.

Creative dialogue is crucial to your becoming energized and innovative. Here are some of the actions you can take now to make sure this happens.

Broaden and widen the topics. To have creative dialogue, you want to converse with people who are interesting and exciting and who are able to converse on broad and wide topics.

Actions to take now to broaden and widen the topics of conversation

Action 2.6 *Broadening the topics of conversation.* Many of the previous actions are about putting aside time in your schedule for one-on-one conversations with others. Now think about how you are going to spend that time, and decide in advance the questions you want to discuss and also some interesting ideas or information you would like to bring to the conversation. Take a look at Action 5, Jumping out of the Boundaries That Constrain You, to see how you might broaden and widen conversations by forming associations with people who are very different from you (see Chapter Eleven).

Beware of spell breakers. Creative dialogues arise when the topics are crucial to you and your colleagues and when you are feeling positive and engaged. The conversation among Barbara, Adam, and Ramona worked so well precisely because each of them really cared. Adam cared about increasing the range of the product, Barbara cared about serving the customers, and Ramona cared deeply about the coffee growers. Each of them had a personal engagement with the topic. Conversely, there is nothing more effective at destroying the quality of conversations than indifference and cynicism—people who drift in and out physically or intellectually, who remain superficial, who break the spell. It is not easy to remain positive and in the moment at all times in these conversations. And I am sure you know people who, when they enter a room, bring down the energy and enthusiasm of everyone present.

Actions to take now to avoid the spell breakers

Action 2.7   *Neutralizing spell breakers.* Highly negative people have to be kept away, lest their negative contribution prevent creative dialogues from occurring.

- First, identify your spell breakers. Think back over the last six months to conversations you have had that have left you feeling deflated. Who participated in these conversations? If the same names come up again and again, you have found your spell breakers.

- Next, work out a strategy to avoid the spell breakers in your everyday life. This can be as simple as walking on the other side of the corridor, making sure you don't linger with them after a meeting, or remembering not to stand next to them at a social event.

So what happens if your spell breaker is your boss? Now it gets a little trickier. Here are three ideas:

- Neutralize your boss's negative energy by always being upbeat and positive when you are together and keeping your conversation to a minimum.

- If you are up to it, use this as an opportunity to practice your emotional skills by asking questions like "Why can't we work together?"

- If all else fails, take a very close look at Action 3, acting on the "smell of the place."

Key Points in Chapter Six

ACTION 2

Mastering the Art of Great Conversation

People who *Glow*, and the Hot Spots they inhabit, abound with great conversation—and great conversation is what ties you together as you cooperate with others. So if you want to *Glow* by finding, creating, and flourishing in Hot Spots, you must examine how you converse with others.

Great conversations have elements of both analytical rationality and emotional authenticity.

Dehydrated Talk
Dehydrated talk results when you have neither analytical rationality nor emotional authenticity.

Disciplined Debate
Disciplined debate uses high-quality information to move the conversation forward.

Action 2.1   Asking rigorous and disciplined questions

Action 2.2   Finding high-quality information

Intimate Exchange
Intimate exchange brings emotional authenticity to conversations and is crucial to conversations that *Glow*.

Action 2.3   Devoting time to conversation

Action 2.4   Having wide-ranging conversations

Action 2.5   Asking emotional questions

Creative Dialogue

Creative dialogue results when analytical rationality and emotional authenticity are brought together to create important and meaningful conversations.

Action 2.6   Broadening the topics of conversation

Action 2.7   Neutralizing spell breakers

Chapter Seven

ACTION 3

Acting on the "Smell of the Place"

People who Glow are astute at acting on the "smell of the place." They know the signs of the Big Freeze and how to avoid them and take action to ensure that they move to teams and communities where cooperation flourishes.

Sometimes you have no choice: if you want to *Glow*, you may have to be prepared to move, to put yourself in a different place with different people. To do that you have to become skilled at understanding and acting on the "smell of the place." The "smell of the place" consists of all those subtle clues that tell you intuitively and rationally what a place is like before you join. Being aware of the "smell of the place" will help you find teams, communities, and companies that will help you *Glow* and avoid those that won't.

Remember that *Glowing* is a lot about you, but it is also about the company you keep. That's what Gareth found in his work experience. Recall that Gareth is a young man who from an early age has been trained to adopt the habits of cooperation. When he left college, he was lucky enough to join a company that supported and cherished his cooperative attitude and reinforced and built his cooperative skills. I do believe that luck was involved because my guess is that Gareth had little idea of what he was letting himself in for at the time. So when he switched companies, he was in for a big shock. Not only did his colleagues fail to behave cooperatively with him, they even went so far as to exploit his goodwill. Gareth had joined a place that was playing to a complete different set of rules than those he was used to—and he was coming out as the loser. Gareth had failed to pick up on the "smell of the place," which was distinctly competitive, before he took the job.

Gareth was experiencing one of the worst forms of cooperative misalignment: a cooperative person surrounded by others who are motivated solely by self-interest. Under such circumstances, he was doomed to be treated unfairly. Of course, you could say that the moral of the story is that it is smart to be self-interested when you are with others who are also self-interested. The problem is that being self-interested will significantly reduce your capacity to *Glow* and, in the longer run, your innovation and success.

What is clear from Gareth's story is that the alignment of the three resources of your work life really matters. If you develop cooperative attitudes, habits, and skills, you will not flourish in a self-interested, highly competitive business. So you need to become sensitized to highly competitive teams and businesses—and avoid them.

How are you going to do that? Obviously, you don't want to end up like Gareth, surrounded by self-interested people without realizing what he was getting himself into. What you need is a strategy for choosing a team and a business to work with.

Here is a strategy to help you to understand and act on the "smell of the place." The point is to ask a set of questions before you decide to join. By asking these questions, you are gathering sufficient information to get a handle on the culture of the place and the attitudes toward cooperation—the "smell of the place." By asking these questions, you put yourself on a more equal footing with prospective employers and can gain an understanding of what you might be in for.

The Three Questions That Identify the "Smell of the Place"

These are the questions you should answer before you decide to join a team, a community, or a company.

First Question: Is the Language of the Place Cooperative or Competitive?

The language of the place is an important aspect of the "smell of the place" and in this case the "sound of the place." So listen very carefully to the words that are used to describe the company and the language executives and employees use.

Begin by engaging in an Internet search on how the executives of the business describe themselves and how the media and analysts describe the company. If Gareth had done this before joining the second company, he would have found the following excerpts from the business press:

> *... an aggressive company, the brainchild of the two founders—expect sparks to fly ... a take-no-prisoners culture, built from a ruthless obsession with the bottom line ... known to show no mercy to competitors ...*

Every word used to describe this company suggests the opposite of cooperation. Aggressive, ruthless, no mercy—all are words that would have alerted Gareth to the "smell of the place." By looking closely at what analysts and commentators said about the company, Gareth would have concluded that this is a place where cooperation is unlikely to flourish.

Furthermore, if he had read the CEO's statement in the annual report, he would have seen this statement: "I believe this is a war we have to win; we are in the midst of a furious battle." Again, the place sounds competitive, describing its business with words like war, win, and battle. If you want to find a company where cooperation flourishes, look for a CEO who uses words like partnership, fairness, and community when describing the company and who uses *we* far more often than *I*.

☼ *Actions to take now to analyze the language of the place*

Action 3.1   *Analyzing the language of the place.* Next time you are thinking about changing companies or finding a new job, search for what analysts say about the company and what the CEO or other executives say in press releases and annual reports.

- Count how many times they use competitive words (war, battles, losers, winners) and how many times they use cooperative words (partnership, cooperation, team).

- Use your sense of the "smell of the place" to avoid highly competitive places and find cooperative places.

Second Question: How Well Does the Executive Team Work Together?

Next, you can get a sense of the "smell of the place" before you join by observing how the executive team works together. The executives' day-to-day interactions will give you some important clues as to what you can expect with regard to cooperation. Cooperative companies and communities have teams who work cooperatively with each other; the Big Freeze often comes with teams who are at war with each other.

So what Gareth should have done to get the "smell of the place" was to read any reports he could get his hands on indicating how the senior executives work with one another. This would have given him an important insight into whether a culture of cooperation prevailed. It would also have given him an idea as to whether there would be cooperative coaches and mentors available to support him after he joined. Had he done this, he would have found comments in the press like these:

> *a highly competitive team, often involved in boardroom tussles . . . renowned for its turnover—in fact, the last two heads of operations were summarily fired . . .*

With this sort of information, Gareth would have realized that this was not a cooperative place to work, and was a place where he was unlikely to gain access to a mentor.

⁙ *Actions to take now to analyze how executives work together*

Action 3.2 *Analyzing the press.* Take a look at press coverage of the company over the past year, and see if you can find three or four articles about the senior executives and how they work as a team.

- First, assess the extent to which commentators and analysts describe the company as internally competitive. For example, do they describe the executives as "warriors" or write about "boardroom battles"?

- Next, consider the length of time senior executives stay in their positions before they are fired or move on. If executive turnover is high, this gives you a clue about the "smell of the place."

- If commentators use competitive language to describe the company and executive turnover is high, you can assume it is a competitive place and not one that will enable you to *Glow.*

Third Question: Will I Be Treated in a Way That Fosters Cooperation?

Finally, you will need to take a close look at the way in which people in the company are treated—before you take the job. For example, you will want to consider how pay awards are determined, how selection takes place (reflect on the process they have so far used with you), how people are promoted and trained. Here are four specific questions you can legitimately ask:

How will my pay be determined? Companies where there is little emphasis on supporting cooperative behavior tend to place a great deal of emphasis on paying individual "stars." On the face of it, this may sound attractive. The danger is that an overemphasis on individual performance rather than group performance works strongly against people cooperating with one another. In cooperative companies there will be a greater balance between paying for the performance of the individual and the performance of the team.

On what basis will I be promoted? The choices around how promotion takes place are a crucial signal to the "smell of the place." Cooperative cultures tend to focus on gathering information from a wide range of colleagues and peers before making promotion decisions. At the bank Goldman Sachs, renowned for its internal culture of cooperation, the views of at least twenty peers and colleagues are systematically heard before a promotion to a senior position is made. In soliciting the views of peers and colleagues, the emphasis is on discovering to what extent the candidate for promotion is able and skilled at working both with colleagues on his or her team and with colleagues in other functions and company businesses.

Will I be mentored? I have discovered that one of the most important signs of a cooperative company is that senior executives are prepared to give their time to mentor others. At the communications and data company Reuters, for example, mentoring is a two-way process. Senior executives mentor younger members of the firm on business strategy and market conditions. At the same time, younger members mentor senior executives (even CEO Tom Glaser) in the latest trends in technology. These networks for mentoring relationships signal to potential new joiners that Reuters is likely to be a place where they will experience a cooperative culture.

Will I have an opportunity to engage with the wider community? Companies that emphasize working with the outside community are more likely to be cooperative inside. An example of this would be eBay employees, who for many years have worked closely with villages in South America. Members of the company provide the skills and resources to help these villages have access to the computing skills that will give them access to global marketplaces for their goods. By working cooperatively outside the company, executives are learning the habits of cooperation that they can take back with them into the company.

✺ *Actions to take now to analyze whether the company supports cooperation*

Action 3.3   *Asking questions before joining.* Before you take your next job, ask four questions about the company:

- How will I be paid? Is there some team or community aspect of the way in which pay is determined?

- How will I be promoted? Are people promoted on the basis of their competence as team members, coaches, and mentors?

- What are the opportunities for me to be mentored?

- Will I get the chance to support the community?

Armed with insights from these three broad questions about language, senior executive behavior, and people practices, you will be in a much stronger position to determine before you join a company whether it is a place where cooperation flourishes. Of course, you may decide that despite having determined that this is a place where cooperation does not flourish, you still wish to join. That's your prerogative. Just be aware that you will have to work especially hard if you want to *Glow*.

Key Points in Chapter Seven

ACTION 3

Acting on the "Smell of the Place"

Sometimes you have no choice—if you want to *Glow*, you may have to be prepared to move your job to a different place with different people. To make sure you join a place that will encourage you to *Glow*, you have to become skilled at understanding and acting on the "smell of the place"—those subtle clues that tell you intuitively and rationally what this place is like before you join. That will help you find teams, communities, and companies that will encourage you to *Glow* and avoid those that won't.

Before you join a new business, community, or company, get answers to these three questions:

First Question: Is the Language of the Place Cooperative or Competitive?

Action 3.1   Analyzing the language of the place

Second Question: How Well Does the Senior Team Work Together?

Action 3.2   Analyzing the press

Third Question: Will I Be Treated in a Way That Fosters Cooperation?

Action 3.3   Asking questions before joining

Armed with insights from these three broad questions, you will be in a much stronger position to determine before you join a company whether it is a place where cooperation flourishes.

Chapter Eight

The Second Principle: Jumping Across Worlds

When your relationships with other people are built on cooperation, trust, and appreciation, you have the tantalizing possibility of undertaking extraordinary endeavors and *Glowing*. However, it's not just your relationships with your closest colleagues that are so crucial. Think more broadly of the vast cloud of acquaintances, friends, and friends of friends who surround you. Recent estimates suggest that in modern societies, many adults have thousands of acquaintances, of which about one hundred can be contacted immediately to help out. Of these hundreds of acquaintances, you probably keep in regular contact with about twenty people, of whom perhaps three are close confidants. So when you think about how to *Glow* and to create, find, or flourish in a Hot Spot, think about the vast cloud of people you have to support you.

Recall the way that Frank was able to reach out into his network when faced with a particularly thorny task—and how Fred failed because he closed down rather than opened up.

In exploring this second principle, you will see what it means to make your network work for you—to jump across worlds. You will begin with a story from my town in Spain and then learn more about why variety of thought can be so exciting. Then you will complete the *Glow* Profile for jumping across worlds and hear how a group of people created extraordinary energy and innovation by being prepared and able to jump across worlds. Finally, you will take a closer look at the three actions that are crucial to your jumping across worlds.

Action 4 Being skilled at *increasing the value of your networks* and balancing your networks between acquaintances and close friends—who are similar to you—with broader connections to people who are very different from you. To understand that sometimes the most interesting and most innovative ideas come from people whom you barely know and who are very different from you.

Action 5 *Broadening and extending your networks by being skilled at jumping across the boundaries that constrain you.* Allowing serendipity in your life and being prepared to meet new people and take the untrodden path to broaden your experiences.

Action 6 *Being adept at finding and moving to boundaryless places,* knowing how to avoid the traps of the Fortress and instead finding teams and places to work that encourage and enable you to jump across boundaries.

When I asked people like Frank who *Glow* what it meant to jump across worlds, this is what they said of their experiences:

> "*I really appreciated working with people who were completely different from me.*"

> "*I enjoyed being in a new situation with new people.*"

> "*What really excited me was that I was able to make time for people outside of my normal group.*"

> "*I was suddenly confronted with ideas completely different from my own—I felt exuberant and energized.*"

The opposite is Fred's experience. Instead of opening up and reaching out, he closed down and became a Fortress. This is how people described being in a Fortress:

"I felt I was hearing the same old stuff over and over again."

"I felt as if I had 'bunkered down.'"

"It seemed that the walls around me were so high I just could not jump over them."

"It was a real 'us and them' mentality."

"We became very suspicious of strangers."

It's easy to build walls around us—they can make us feel safe. The problem is that a Fortress is as much a prison for those inside as it is a protection. Fortresses can keep you safe—but sometimes jumping out of them can make you feel great and open you up to new ideas and innovation. To illustrate this, let me tell you a little story about a time when I *Glowed*.

When Two Worlds Meet: A Chocolate Story

Much of my thinking and writing takes place in my house in Spain. The town that surrounds me is an easygoing place where I tend to bump into people who are rather different from me. My opportunities to meet others are helped enormously by the lack of cars in the town and the number of pedestrian streets. I, like many of my neighbors, do not have a car and travel everywhere in town on foot. The combination of the warm Mediterranean climate, the streets filled with walkers, the numerous tapas bars where lighthearted banter takes place, and the rather odd mix of people seemingly blown from across the globe makes this a wonderful place for just roaming and conversing. When I am in this town, I become what the French writer Baudelaire called a *flâneur*. This is a wanderer, a person who simply walks around a city with little idea of where the journey will take them, being simply interested and inquisitive. As a consequence of my being a *flâneur* in my small town, I tend to spend my time with people who are very different from the people I meet in London, where the gray skies, dense traffic, and isolated homes seem to serve as barriers to my meeting people different from me.

So imagine for a moment me walking one fine morning through the narrow cobblestone streets of this medieval town, smiling and chatting as

I buy my bread and drink my coffee. During my morning journey, I meet a friend who invites me to have coffee with some friends of hers. One of these people I then have coffee with (having coffee seems to be important to the life of a *flâneur*) is Oriol Balaguer, a man from Barcelona who is rapidly building a reputation for himself as one of the most creative chocolate makers of his generation.

So here I am in Spain, jumping across worlds. I am jumping from my normal world of academics and book writers into quite a different one, the world of chocolate makers. When two completely different worlds like these collide, the results can be great fun, very innovative, and wonderful opportunities to *Glow*. At the time I met Oriol, I was thinking about the principles at the heart of Hot Spots and of *Glow*. As a result of our collision of worlds, I am today the proud purveyor of chocolates that symbolize the principles of *Glow*! In each box there are four gorgeous chocolates, each filled with a center flavored with an ingredient reminiscent of the *Glow* principles: the sweetness of cooperation (flavored with vanilla), the surprise of jumping across worlds (flavored with sea salt), the power of ignition (flavored with wasabi mustard), and finally a chocolate that has a filling which seems to explode in your mouth—creating a wonderful sense of *Glow*. It's a small episode in my path to *Glowing*, but it neatly illustrates how jumping across worlds can bring both joy and innovation. I have great fun when I talk about energy and innovation to groups of people and ask them to eat the corresponding chocolate as we talk of each principle. Who can easily forget a concept like Hot Spots and *Glowing* when you have thought about it, talked about it, and tasted it all at the same time!

For me this is a classic case of creating the conditions to *Glowing*. I had time to wander (unusual in my normal high-paced London schedule but more likely in my Spanish sojourns), and I was in a context that encouraged me to meet unusual people.

Over and over I have discovered that to *Glow* you need to give yourself time to seek out people who are on the borders of their own world and on the thresholds of other worlds. Like me in my Mediterranean town, people who *Glow* do so by discovering fascinating people as they move around, and by meeting people by pure chance. And it's not simply people like me, who often work from home, who can learn to *Glow*; as you will discover, even the most hierarchical organization offers opportunities to reach out to others.

> *Encounters between people who are very different from each other but prepared to trust and cooperate are where the interesting stuff happens.*

These new ideas rarely surface if you simply stay in your own world, with people who are similar to you and with whom you are close friends.

What's Going On in Your Head? A Word About Variety

What happens when you jump across worlds? Why was it that Oriol and I, and others who are prepared to jump across worlds, feel that we are *Glowing*? Often when you work with other people who are very similar to you, you go through a process of homogenization whereby you both become more and more similar and end up with mediocre and average ideas. However, when you jump across worlds, each person can contribute something unique. It is this combination of "uniquenesses" that is the magic of Hot Spots—and what lets you *Glow*.

To understand more about this combination of uniquenesses, let's go back to me and the chocolate maker Oriol. Each of us has our own unique way of looking at the world. We have our own way of seeing situations and our own way of interpreting what we see; we can then generate our own unique solutions to problems (this has been termed *heuristics*); and we have our own unique way of predicting what we believe will happen.

Let's take a closer look at heuristics. If you think about your life and your work you will see that over time you have created a way of looking at your world and deciding to act in it. These ways of looking—or heuristics—are developed through your past experiences. So your heuristics are influenced by such factors as whether you are a man or a women, your culture and the country you have grown up in, your religious beliefs, and your education. They are also influenced by your life experiences and what you have learned from others. Your personally developed rules and ways of acting become the rules you use to define your world. Heuristics can range in sophistication from simple rules of thumb—"if you feel cold, put on more clothes"—to more sophisticated—"this is how you go about editing a book."

The impact of heuristics on creating Hot Spots and learning to *Glow* can be described in this way:

> *The more cognitively diverse the collection of heuristics, the better able you and others are to create Hot Spots of innovation and energy and to Glow.*

Note that a diverse collection of heuristics is not always what you need. For example, you don't need cognitive diversity if you are deciding how to mop the floor or serve burgers. But when your work is complex—as it often is—then cultivating diverse networks trumps just staying close to your own group who are similar to you. It pays to jump across worlds.

To get a better idea of what this means to you, let's play this out and see how it evolves. I am going to begin with a very simple example, and then we can circle back to the example of the chocolates.

Let's imagine that I am working with a colleague at London Business School. Professor Rob Goffee and I have been asked to create a new leadership program. As we begin to share ideas, both Rob and I are bringing our own perspectives about situations, our own unique ways of interpreting what we see, of generating solutions to problems, and of predicting what we believe will happen. Let's imagine that I bring seven heuristics to the challenge of designing a new leadership program. (By the way, the figure seven is not arbitrary; research reveals that seven is the number of heuristics we typically work with.) Let's call my seven heuristics

A B C D E F G

For example, heuristic A is a heuristic I use that is a rule of thumb whereby I assume that senior executives like to mix with their peers—so when in the past I have designed an executive training program, I always make sure I bring business leaders to present to participants.

Now let's consider what heuristics Rob will be bring to the problem. Like me, he has a doctorate, we are about the same age, we both write books, and we are both British. There are two major differences between us—Rob is a man, and he is trained as a sociologist; I am a woman and am trained as a psychologist. The heuristic set that Rob brings can be defined as

$$B\ C\ D\ E\ F\ G\ H$$

Thus Rob and I share many of the same rules of thumb about how to proceed with the design of the leadership program. However, Rob does not have heuristic A (senior executives like to mix with their peers), but he does have heuristic H, which I don't. Heuristic H says that successful executive programs build networks back into the executive's workplace—so when in the past Rob has designed an executive program, he always makes sure he uses 360-degree feedback.

Now let's imagine that Rob and I are working together to design the program. Our combined heuristics would look like this:

Lynda's heuristics:	$A\ B\ C\ D\ E\ F\ G$
Rob's heuristics:	$B\ C\ D\ E\ F\ G\ H$
Lynda and Rob's heuristics:	$A\ B\ C\ D\ E\ F\ G\ H$

So when Rob and I work together, we each bring one unique heuristic (I bring A and Rob brings H), and together we have eight heuristics. That means that as we proceed, we have a broader perspective than if we worked completely on our own. That's why *teams* of relatively savvy people almost always come up with better solutions to a problem than a *single expert*. The question is whether Rob and I are sufficiently different from each other to really *Glow* as we work together. It's possible, but it's unlikely that we would create a real Hot Spot of energy and innovation around this task, simply because we are too similar. So although we will find it very easy to work with each other thanks to our similarities, chances are we will produce something that is similar to programs we have designed before. We will both stay in our similar worlds and are unlikely to achieve the creativity or innovation of a Hot Spot.

Now let's take another look at the challenge of designing an executive program. This time, instead of pairing me with Rob, let's pair me with Oriol, the chocolate maker from Barcelona. Recall that he has been trained in chocolate, is Spanish, works in a highly creative community in Barcelona, and is an entrepreneur. So let's describe the heuristics by which he lives his life as

G J K L M N O

Oriel's heuristic G says that you should be as creative as you can whenever possible.

Now let's imagine that Oriol and I began to get to know each other and decided we wanted to work together to develop a really innovative way of developing leaders. The combination of heuristics we would bring to the task is as follows:

Lynda's heuristics:	A B C D E F G
Oriol's heuristics:	G J K L M N O
Lynda and Oriol's heuristics:	A B C D E F G J K L M N O

We both share a heuristic about being creative (G), but in all other ways, we are completely different—in fact, together we bring thirteen heuristics to bear on the problem. The bad news, of course, is that because Oriol and I have so little in common, it may be difficult for us to relate to and understand each other, and Oriol has no experience whatsoever in the task at hand. That's why the skills for jumping across worlds, which we will explore in Action 5 (Chapter Eleven), are so crucial. But imagine how exciting it would be if Oriol and I could find an igniting vision or question toward which we could both work! The result we could come up with would be so much more interesting. The good news of the thirteen heuristics is that faced with a complex task, a big question, or an exciting vision (all crucial for the ignition of

Glow), these thirteen heuristics provide a broader spread of possibilities than the set of seven heuristics each of us brought to the task.

The lessons from this short foray into heuristics are clear: you should seek out people with diverse experiences, training, and identities that translate into diverse perspectives and heuristics. To do this, you have to be able to jump across worlds.

The Glow Profile

Before we take a closer look at developing the requisite abilities, complete the jumping across worlds portion of the *Glow* Profile to gain a deeper understanding of your current situation.

Profiling the Second Principle: Jumping Across Worlds

The rating scales in Figure 8.1 will help you determine your own beliefs regarding jumping across worlds, how the members of your immediate team or community work together, and how your wider community, business, or organization behaves.

Respond to each statement by circling your reaction on the 5-point scale, as follows:

5 = agree completely
4 = agree somewhat
3 = neither agree nor disagree
2 = disagree somewhat
1 = disagree completely

Once you have responded to all the statements in Figure 8.1, add up your ratings in each section; they will range from 9 to 45.

36 to 45 = high
26 to 35 = moderate
 9 to 27 = low

Do I naturally jump across worlds?

- I have worked in more than one business in my career.   5 4 3 2 1
- I have worked in more than one country in my career.   5 4 3 2 1
- I have worked in more than one function in my career.   5 4 3 2 1
- I always try to meet people outside my immediate work group.   5 4 3 2 1
- It is important to me that I have networks outside the company.   5 4 3 2 1
- I really enjoy being with people who are different from me.   5 4 3 2 1
- I am good at appreciating differences in others.   5 4 3 2 1
- I enjoy joining communities outside of work.   5 4 3 2 1
- I like to leave time for the unexpected.   5 4 3 2 1

Does my team naturally jump across worlds?

- The people on my team are from many different backgrounds.   5 4 3 2 1
- On my team, it is normal to seek ideas from outside the team.   5 4 3 2 1
- Members of my team often introduce me to people in their
  wider network.   5 4 3 2 1
- On our team, we really appreciate the differences between us.   5 4 3 2 1
- Our team works closely with people from other functions or
  businesses.   5 4 3 2 1
- On my team, partnerships with people outside the company are
  very important.   5 4 3 2 1
- On my team, it is normal to take time to meet other people.   5 4 3 2 1
- On my team, we work hard to communicate what we do with
  the wider community.   5 4 3 2 1
- Members of my team are always looking for ways to broaden
  their networks.   5 4 3 2 1

Is my wider community, business, or organization naturally boundaryless?

- People are encouraged to work closely with people on other teams. 5 4 3 2 1
- It is the norm for people to have careers that go across more than
  one function or business.   5 4 3 2 1
- My boss encourages me to meet people from other parts of the
  business.   5 4 3 2 1
- Executives make it a point to introduce me to their networks.   5 4 3 2 1
- Part of my pay is dependent on whether I have worked with
  other teams.   5 4 3 2 1
- There are many opportunities to share knowledge with the
  wider community.   5 4 3 2 1
- We are encouraged to join networks related to our areas of interest. 5 4 3 2 1
- There are many opportunities, such as conferences and workshops,
  for me to associate with people from other parts of the business.   5 4 3 2 1
- We are encouraged to develop strong working relationships with
  suppliers and partners.   5 4 3 2 1

FIGURE 8.1 Jumping Across Worlds in the Three Areas of Your Work Life

The *Glow* Profile

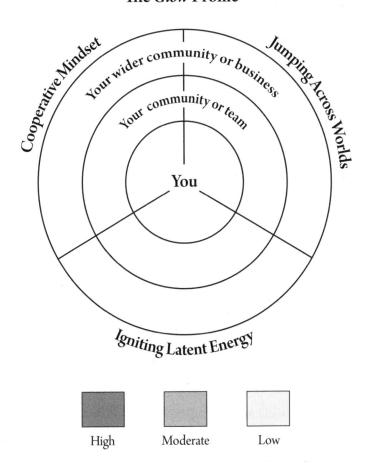

High   **Moderate**   **Low**

FIGURE 8.2 Your Jumping Across Worlds Profile

Now move to the *Glow* Profile in Figure 8.2. In the "jumping across worlds" segment of the figure, use different colors or a coding scheme such as the one shown to indicate the extent of jumping across boundaries in the three areas of your work life.

Interpreting the Jumping Across Worlds Profile

Take a look at your jumping across worlds profile, and select the type that is closest to yours.

Profile Type	Your Score	Team or Community Score	Wider Community Score
A	High	High	High
B	Moderate or High	Moderate	Moderate
C	Moderate or High	Low	Low
D	Low	Moderate or High	Moderate or High
E	Low	Low	Low

Profile Type A: Your score for jumping across worlds is high, and so are the scores for the team and the community

You are a natural at jumping across worlds. You instinctively take a broad view of the world, and you have developed the skills of appreciating others and working with people who are different from you. You will work well in a Hot Spot and have the potential to *Glow* brightly

Your natural capabilities for jumping across worlds are reflected in your team or community, which has a boundaryless way of looking at the world and has developed the skills of establishing broad networks and working with people who differ in many respects.

Your organization or business is also a naturally boundaryless place where people are comfortable with diversity. Senior executives support others to establish broad networks and are prepared to introduce people across the various worlds of the company. The organization has also developed practices and processes, such as the way they manage careers and pay, that encourage people to jump across worlds.

Actions to Take You are in a great situation and have a wonderful opportunity to *Glow* and to find and flourish in Hot Spots. Review Actions 4, 5, and 6 (Chapters Ten, Eleven and Twelve) to ensure that there is not more you could be doing. Your main action is to look at your analysis of cooperative mindset to ensure that you have sufficient cooperation to make the most of these networks and at your analysis of igniting latent energy to be sure that the potential energy of jumping across worlds is able to be ignited.

Profile Type B: Your score for jumping across worlds is moderate or high, and the team and community scores are moderate

If your score is moderate, your skill at jumping across worlds could be more developed, but you have the potential to master it, and taking action can develop this potential. If your score is high, you already have well-developed capabilities in this area. Take a look at Action 5 with your colleagues (see Chapter Eleven) and as a group determine the one or two actions that will make a real difference.

Actions to Take   You have the great advantage of being a natural at jumping across worlds and now need to engage with others to encourage them to become more capable. Your first action is to engage them with these concepts—join with your colleagues as a learning group and discuss how to become more boundaryless.

Profile Type C: Your score for jumping across worlds is moderate or high, and the team and community scores are low

You are a natural at jumping across worlds, you have a naturally broad way of looking at the world, and you have developed the skills of appreciating others and working with people who are different from you. However, you are closed up in a Fortress where the people around you don't celebrate working with different types of people and developing networks outside the group.

Actions to Take   You can support the team by sharing these diagnostics and engaging in Action 5 (see Chapter Eleven). Or you can choose to work less with this team and find projects and teams that are more boundaryless or a wider community or organization that is more in sync with your own values. If you decide to take this action, explore Action 6, finding and moving to boundaryless places (see Chapter Twelve).

Profile Type D: Your score for jumping across worlds is low, and the team and community scores are moderate or high

Until now, you have not valued working across boundaries and jumping across worlds. But by remaining like this, you face the possibility of narrowing your options and reducing your capacity to be innovative and ultimately to *Glow*.

However, you now find yourself in a place where the people around you are prepared and willing to take a chance and jump out of their immediate networks. You have an opportunity to watch what they do and learn from their habits and skills.

Actions to Take   You are in a great position to build your boundaryless skills and habits because you have around you people who work across networks. So take a closer look at Action 4 (Chapter Ten) to see how your current network is playing out—and what competencies you need to develop now to support broader networks. Then look at Action 5 (Chapter Eleven) to identify the specific actions you can take to find activities that will build your capabilities for jumping across worlds.

Profile Type E: Your score for jumping across worlds is low, and so are the scores for the team and the community

Have you noticed that you are becoming isolated from people outside your immediate group? The challenge is that it will be difficult for you to create Hot Spots of energy or innovation and to *Glow* because you don't meet enough interesting people to spark your imagination. Your team has very strong internal boundaries, and the focus is inward rather than outward. If you try to breach these boundaries, you may be branded as a traitor and not supportive of the team. This is a team that could very significantly reduce your capacity to *Glow*.

Actions to Take   First, you have to build your own capabilities for jumping across worlds. Take a look at Action 4, increasing the value of your networks (Chapter Ten), and Action 5, jumping out of the boundaries that constrain you (Chapter Eleven), to see how you can do this. Then you have two choices: stay and work on reducing the boundaries, or find a more receptive team. If you decide to leave, take a close look at Action 6, finding and moving to boundaryless places (Chapter Twelve), to make sure you don't make the same mistake again.

Key Points in Chapter Eight

The Second Principle: Jumping Across Worlds

To *Glow*, you need the excitement and energy of meeting people who are very different from you. The story of the chocolates illustrated the innovation that can come out of very different people meeting in a cooperative way. When people meet, they bring their own ways of looking at the world (heuristics). It is this cognitive diversity that can create unique combinations.

In this chapter the *Glow* Profile helped you see where you stand with regard to your own attitudes and skills, your team's attitudes and competence, and the extent to which your company or community encourages you to jump across worlds. From the profile you are able to determine which profile type is nearest to your own:

Profile Type A   You, the team you work with, and your wider community are very adept at jumping across worlds and creating boundaryless conditions, which creates a marvelous foundation for you to *Glow*.

Profile Type B   You, your team, and the wider community are skilled in some aspects of jumping across worlds, which suggests that Action 5, jumping out of the boundaries that constrain you, will be crucial.

Profile Type C   You are fairly adept at jumping across worlds but find yourself in a Fortress with high walls , which suggests that you need to think seriously about taking Action 5, jumping out of the boundaries that constrain you

Profile Type D You are not a natural at jumping across worlds but find yourself surrounded by a relatively boundaryless team or community, which presents a terrific opportunity for you to learn from others. Take a look at Actions 4 and 5 to determine how to increase the value of your networks and to create more boundaryless working.

Profile Type E Neither you, your team, nor the larger community values jumping across worlds, which places you in a Fortress. Think about the effect this is having, particularly on innovation, and together work on all three actions to increase the value of your networks and create a place that is more boundaryless and encourages reaching out to others.

Chapter Nine

Chocolate Stories and Connecting Different Worlds

Jumping across worlds can be a marvelous creator of the energy of *Glow*; in Chapter Eight you heard my story of bringing together chocolates and writing. Here is another story, this one about how Harry and his colleagues learned to *Glow* and create a Hot Spot. As you read the story, think about how the networks in your working life have sometimes created wonderful moments of joy and excitement.

Harry's Story

I am a manager at Unilever, and I work on the Lynx deodorant brand. Let's face it, this is a tough market to work in. There are hundreds of brands of deodorant out there, all competing for a space on the supermarket shelves, and profits are razor-thin. Sometimes I feel pretty down about how I am ever going to be able to succeed as a manager and really bring energy and innovation to my work. But last year was one of those great times when I really felt as if I was making a difference—I really felt I was *Glowing*. Here is how it all started.

At the beginning of the year I attended one of Unilever's one-week strategy development programs at the company's management training center. A bunch of us from my team went along, and we spent much of the time together. However, at one dinner I found myself sitting next to Julie. She is a manager for the Walls confectionery line. We began to chat that evening and agreed to meet again the next day.

It was one of those great conversations. We talked about the challenges we both faced in our product lines and the marketplace. Then we began to talk about our families and our teenage children. It did not take long for us to realize that we both have teenage boys with some of the same obsessions—girls and football! As we met over the course of the week, I really opened up to her about my concerns about the deodorant market, particularly the market for teenagers like ours. Teenagers are notoriously fickle and quick to move to whatever brand is the hippest at the moment.

At the end of the program, Julie invited me to come to the Walls development center to meet with her team. It was a great meeting. I was really amazed to hear about some of the groundbreaking work going on at Walls with respect to flavorings—particularly their research on chocolate. The Walls premium product, the Magnum brand, is one of the company's top-selling ice-cream lines, and Julie introduced me to her colleague Angela, who is developing a range of chocolates to be launched under the Magnum brand. Later that day I was introduced to Robert, who leads the team on chocolate flavoring. He told me all about how difficult it is to create a chocolate essence that smells authentic.

Over the next couple of weeks I really began to trust Julie and thought it would be great to work with her. So we got our teams together and began to think about the teen deodorant market. We began to realize that Julie's team and their insight about creating the essence of chocolate could be a real breakthrough. The moment of greatest creativity came when we combined Julie and her team's knowledge of chocolate with our understanding of the development and marketing of deodorant to teens. The result: a chocolate-scented deodorant body spray for young men!

It was indeed a breakthrough. Once we had the idea, of course, we had to work with each other to thrash out how we could create a high-quality chocolate scent delivered in an aerosol. But you can imagine how great I felt when a year later Lynx's chocolate-scented deodorant, Dark Temptation, was launched and quickly became one of the fastest-selling products aimed at teens that year.

I love Harry's story; he and Julie created a real Hot Spot of energy and innovation that had both of them *Glowing*. By the way, if you don't get the point of a chocolate-smelling deodorant (and I certainly don't!), just ask a teenager why he wants his body to smell like chocolate. I asked my own teenage sons (who were the ones who alerted me to the chocolate deodorant spray in the first place), and they looked at me in amazement: "Girls like chocolate, Mom." Silly me!

Julie and Harry inhabit different worlds—Julie's is the world of research, and Harry lives in the world of marketing. You can picture these worlds with boundaries around them that define who is an insider and who is an outsider. Knowing who's in and who's out brings order and predictability to Harry's and Julie's social relationships. However, if the boundaries become a Fortress and are too rigidly defined, it's going to be much more difficult for them to reach out and jump out or for others to jump in.

Imagine how the story would unfold if people from the Walls business and the Lynx business never meet. Imagine that instead Harry and Julie both work in a big Fortress with insurmountable walls. It would be almost impossible for them to meet each other, and this wonderful Hot Spot would never have been created.

How Jumping Across Worlds Evolves into a Hot Spot

To really understand how Harry and Julie and their teams *Glowed,* let's take another look at the story—but this time tell it as the development of a network of relationships.

We can begin with Harry and his immediate team, made up of John and Joan, both of whom work together on the development of Lynx deodorants for the teenage market. Harry, John, and Joan have worked with one another for years, and they trust each other and have a real sense of achievement about the group. As the network chart in Figure 9.1 shows, John has also built a strong working relationship with Ben, who is on another team that also works on the teenage deodorant market.

John, Harry, and Joan have known each other for years and are very similar, so you can expect their combined heuristic profile to be small—perhaps rather like mine and Rob's in Chapter Eight, where together we managed to bring only eight heuristics. John, Harry, and Joan are about the same age, have roughly similar educational backgrounds, are all British, and all work in the same company. Remember, though, that these similarities have made it easier for them to trust and cooperate with each other.

Reflect for a moment on your own important and significant relationships. Some will have really helped you *Glow,* others will fade into heritage relationships, and still others may fade away completely. In Chapter Ten you will get an opportunity to take a really close look at the types of networks you've developed and to determine whether or not they are helping you *Glow.*

So this little network of Ben, Harry, Joan, and John is working together— everyone feeling good about one another—but not really being innovative. That changed when Harry met Julie at the executive program.

I have found that typically there are two events that can really energize a network and put it on the path to becoming a Hot Spot. One possibility is that as in this case, the variety within the network is expanded when some-

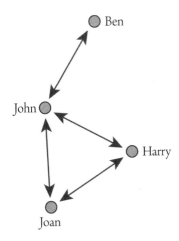

FIGURE 9.1 Harry's Initial Network

one with a different perspective joins. This variety increases the number of heuristics and begins the buzz. The other important event that will transform the warm and trusting relationship to something much more dynamic and exciting is that the latent energy between group members is ignited. In Chapter Thirteen you will see a lot more about how this can happen and learn about what you can do to help it along.

For now, let's concentrate on what happens to this network of relationships as it evolves into a Hot Spot.

The Nascent Hot Spot

Harry's world began to evolve into a Hot Spot when he met Julie at the management conference, and suddenly he began to *Glow*.

When Harry and Julie meet, they are simply acquaintances, so I've shown their relationship in Figure 9.2 as a dotted line. When Harry meets Julie, he is not just meeting her; he has the potential to meet a whole new network. Like Harry, Julie has her own network of close colleagues. Her teammates Robert and Angela are both experts in fragrances and flavors. Note that at this stage Julie and Harry are the only people spanning the

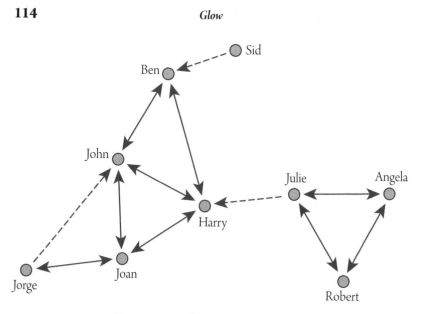

FIGURE 9.2 The Nascent Hot Spot

boundaries between these two worlds—none of the members of their respective networks have yet met.

Harry and Julie have begun the conversation about how they might combine their expertise in chocolate and deodorant. At the same time that Harry talks to Julie, the networks in his own team are also beginning to evolve to include other people like Jorge, who is a friend of Joan's, and Sid, who is an associate of Ben's. The network at this point is shown in Figure 9.2.

What's brought Jorge and Sid into the network is that Harry has become really focused on doing something different. He has asked an igniting question: "What would it take to make a really big difference in the teenage deodorant market?" (You will get an opportunity to rehearse questions that would spark people in your network in Chapter Fourteen.)

Let's trace the evolution of Harry's network:

1. *People jump across worlds.* Harry and Julie meet and begin to talk about what excites and interests them.

2. *The igniting question and task becomes a focus for energy.* The network is transformed into a community of people who are excited about the task.

How to Read a Network Chart

- The lines between people signify that there is a relationship between them.
- Solid arrows signify a strong, trusting relationship.
- Dashed arrows signify a less intense association.
- Some of the less intense associations will be "heritage relationships" that were strong in the past but have now withered. If these heritage relationships are founded on goodwill, they can easily be rekindled.
- The arrows signify the primary direction in which knowledge is shared. When the arrow goes both ways, it signifies that knowledge travels about equally between people. When it goes in one direction, it indicates that one person is the primary giver of knowledge.
- The network diagram shows who are the most prominently connected people within a group.
- The network diagram also reveals who is most adept at jumping across worlds. For example, in the expanded network diagram shown in Figure 9.2, Harry and Julie have reached out to each other and now are both jumping between two distinct groups, the Lynx team and the Walls team.

3. *The initial network expands.* Harry introduces Julie to other people in his network, and Julie introduces Harry and the others to her network. At this early stage, Harry and Julie will be subtly testing each other to see if they can trust each other and cooperate. If they decide to do so, their relationship could strengthen.

4. *The network expands to include people from other countries.* For example, Joan was at college with Jorge, who is now working in California. Jorge has some really good ideas and insights that he is sharing with Joan. Joan has also introduced Jorge to John, and they are also beginning to talk about areas of mutual interest.

5. *The network now extends to people from other communities of practice.* Ben is in another group, which is working on a marketing project

for Generation Y. He brings in Sid who works in a consulting company and like Ben is passionate and really understands the dynamics of Gen Y—people under the age of 27—and has a real focus of attention in the male fragrance market.

You can see this expansion in the network in Figure 9.2—and as the network expands, it builds greater energy and innovation, providing more and more opportunities for Harry and Julie to become innovative and to *Glow*.

In the case of Harry and Julie, this network went on to sparkle and be very creative. That doesn't happen in every case, of course. Sometimes a nascent Hot Spot decays. The initial cooperation and trust between the founding members may come under pressure as more people with many different perspectives and heuristics become involved. Or the nascent Hot Spot may decay as the igniting question or vision loses its capacity to interest and excite people. When decay occurs, by the way, it does not mean that the team inevitably disintegrates and the task goes unfinished. Often the task is completed but becomes more like "business as usual" than a Hot Spot. People engage with it, but not in a high-energy, motivated way.

The Hot Spot

It is astonishing to watch as the Hot Spot gains velocity and energy and more people are interested in getting involved. Some of the people who become involved are already associated with those in the nascent Hot Spot. Others are acquaintances or even strangers, people who have been asked to join the job or the project or task force or have decided to do so of their own volition. It is this combination of founding members, heritage relationships, acquaintances, and relative strangers that bring this wonderful mix of insights, experience, and ideas that fuel the Hot Spot and create a great context for people to *Glow*.

Figure 9.3 shows Harry and Julie's Hot Spot in its most energized form.

1. *Relationships become stronger.* Some initial acquaintances grow into stronger relationships as people share knowledge and develop deeper trust. This was the case with Harry and Julie when they

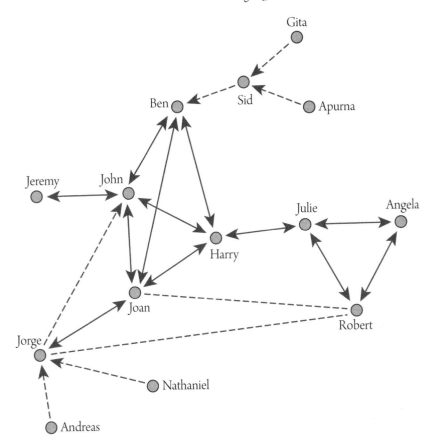

FIGURE 9.3 The Hot Spot

proposed creating a project team that would explore the possible development of a chocolate-smelling spray deodorant. Joan and Ben also established a stronger working relationship as time went on.

2. *People introduce their acquaintances and contacts.* For example, Sid is based in India, so much of his link with the other members of the Hot Spot is virtual. He has introduced Gita and Apurna to the work of the team, and they are also now involved with aspects of it.

3. *People volunteer to join.* This can be a particularly important part of the development of a Hot Spot. In this case, Jorge, who is based

in a research center became so excited about the topic of the Hot Spot that he circulated a note among his graduate students. Two responded (Andreas and Nathaniel), and they are now participants in the Hot Spot—they will contribute what they can and may become more central over time.

When you want to *Glow,* these networks and the ideas and goodwill they generate are going to be crucial to you. So you have to become adept at making them work for you. The actions you will examine in the next three chapters will help you make your networks work for you.

Key Points in Chapter Nine

Chocolate Stories and Connecting Different Worlds

You *Glow* when you have an opportunity to work on exciting projects with people who are very different from you. We began this chapter with a story about how Harry and his colleagues *Glowed* by being excited about a joint project they were engaged in. Harry and Julie came up with the idea of a chocolate-smelling deodorant spray that became a big hit among teenagers. As they worked with their colleagues, a network of relationships evolved into a Hot Spot of energy and innovation.

The *initial network* began with Harry and his immediate work colleagues, who over the years had learned to trust and cooperate with each other.

The *nascent Hot Spot* emerged when Harry met Julie, from a different part of the company. His networks began to change, and two very different groups began to get to know each other.

- People began to jump across worlds.
- The igniting question became a focus of energy.
- The initial network began to expand.

- The network began to draw people in from other countries.

- The network began to extend to people from other communities of practice.

The Hot Spot came to fruition as the community gained velocity, and the energy it provided spurred people to start innovating and *Glowing.* At its most energized point, some of the initial relationships grew much stronger, and people increasingly introduced acquaintances to the network.

Chapter Ten

ACTION 4

Increasing the Value of Your Networks

People who Glow are skilled at increasing the value of their networks and at balancing their networks between acquaintances and close friends who are similar to them with more extensive networks of people who are very different from them. They know that sometimes the most interesting and most innovative ideas come from people whom they barely know and who are very different from them.

Your closest friends are dear to you. It is they who provide the emotional support, warmth, love, and understanding that are so important to your happiness and well-being. It is they who help you through your darkest moments, who know your idiosyncrasies and your foibles.

But if you want to increase your ability to *Glow*, you will have to do more than concentrate on your closest friends. It is natural to keep your friends close, but by focusing too much of your energy on them, you run the risk of severely limiting your capacity to create the sort of energy and innovation Harry did when he reached out to Julie and her network.

The Need for Balance in Your Networks

In this chapter you will see how looking at familiarity and differences in your relationships can help you increase the value of your networks. The key is to achieve a balance of breadth and depth.

> The most valuable strategy you can adopt to increase the value of your networks is to both deepen your relationships and broaden your networks. You need strong, trusting, and highly cooperative friendships, and you need links with a wide variety of associates.

The Power of Deep Relationships

Your closest friends provide emotional support and places where you feel most comfortable and at ease. But this comfort and ease has its downsides. It is possible that you simply talk about the same topics, reinforce each other's views, and protect your friends from hearing things they would find distressing, and vice versa. Your closest friends love you for who and what you are. They want you to remain the same, and they can put pressure on you to be consistent. In other words, although your closest friends and family nurture and support you, if they are your only major networks, they also have the potential to reduce your capacity to explore and to experiment and ultimately to *Glow*. You certainly need your friends, and their love is indispensable to your feelings of self-worth, but you also need to balance this with broader networks of associates.

The Power of Broad and Diverse Networks

You also need many looser connections with people from outside your tight circle of friends. These connections are most powerful when they are with people who are very different from you. These can be people who are from another generation, whose beliefs are different from your own, or who live in different circumstances or in different countries. It is these loose connections, these distant acquaintances, that bring fresh perspectives to your world.

Your time is a precious resource, and to ensure that your networks are valuable, you want to give time to both developing and nurturing your closest friends and creating loose networks with a wide variety of people. For some, particularly people who are natural networkers, widening a network will be second nature. But for others, widening the network can be achieved only in a more deliberate manner.

How Balanced Is Your Network?

We begin exploring this action by taking a closer look at your current networks and evaluating just how balanced they are. To do this, you need to think about the people in your network in two ways:

- How well do we know each other? Is this person an acquaintance or associate, or is the person a close friend of someone with whom we have a strong relationship?

- How different is the person from you? Is this person very similar or very different?

Remember that similarities and differences can come in all sorts of guises. Your friends or acquaintances could be of the same gender, be around your age, share a your religion or culture, come from a similar background, or have a similar profession. Recall from Chapter Nine that Harry and Julie had a lot in common but had completely different work experiences. These similarities are surface similarities, in the sense that you can relatively easily identify gender, age, and so on. However, there are similarities and differences that are much deeper and less obvious yet still very important—for example, points of view, values, or habits. Both surface and deep similarities can act as powerful determinants of the impact of the type and quality of networks you form.

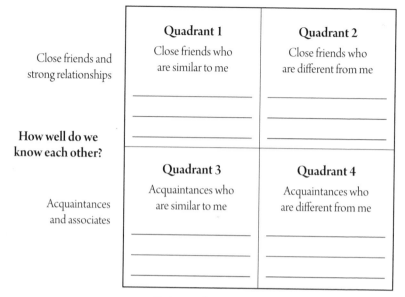

FIGURE 10.1 Analyzing Your Networks

To understand how these two dimensions play out, take a look at Figure 10.1. Take a look at each of the four quadrants and in each quadrant write the names of three people. So in Quadrant 1, identify three people who are close friends who are similar to you; in Quadrant 2, three people who are close friends who are different from you; in Quadrant 3, three people who are acquaintances who are similar to you; and in Quadrant 4, three people who are acquaintances who are different from you. Once you have identified the people in each quadrant, try to give detailed answers to the questions on the axes—"How well do we know each other?" and "How different are we?"—for each person you've identified.

Now that you know more about the people in your networks, the next step is to understand the extent to which these people are adding value to your network and helping you *Glow*.

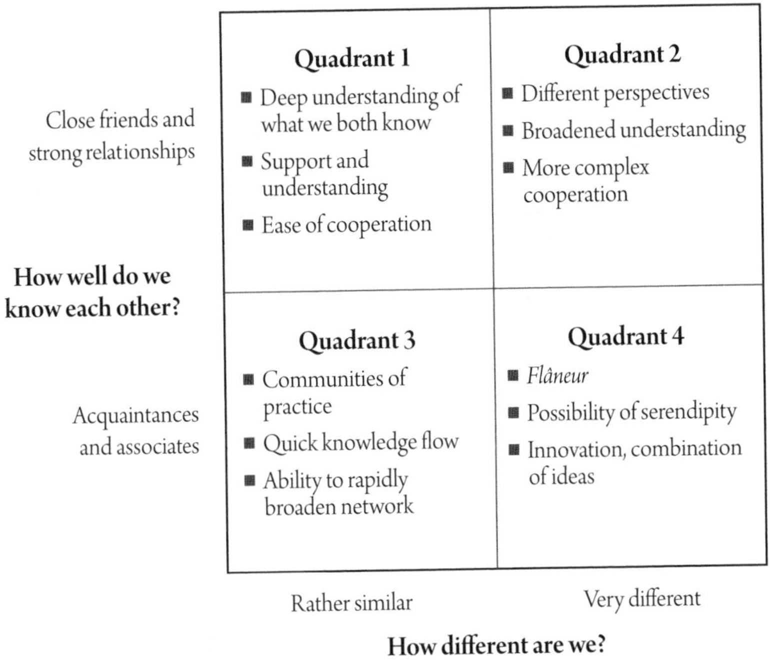

Quadrant 1 ■ Deep understanding of what we both know ■ Support and understanding ■ Ease of cooperation	**Quadrant 2** ■ Different perspectives ■ Broadened understanding ■ More complex cooperation
Quadrant 3 ■ Communities of practice ■ Quick knowledge flow ■ Ability to rapidly broaden network	**Quadrant 4** ■ *Flâneur* ■ Possibility of serendipity ■ Innovation, combination of ideas

Close friends and strong relationships

How well do we know each other?

Acquaintances and associates

Rather similar   Very different

How different are we?

FIGURE 10.2 Potential Value of These Relationships

What Is the Value of Your Networks?

Now for each of the twelve people you've identified, think about how much value they have brought to you, asking yourself questions such as these:

■ Is this a relationship that fills me with joy and helps me *Glow*?

■ Is this a relationship in which I learn new things?

■ Is this a relationship in which I feel cooperative and trusting?

Figure 10.2 shows some of the benefits people typically gain from relationships in the four quadrants. In the descriptions that follow, the actions will give you ideas about how to increase the value of the relationships in each quadrant.

Quadrant 1: Close Friends Who Are Similar to Me

History. These are people you have probably known for some time. You like each other, you have a shared history, and they may well turn out to be founding members of Hot Spots as you create buzz and energy in your work life. Since they are similar to you, the friendship arose with ease, and cooperation between you is second nature.

Value. These are great relationships in which you can understand each other's insights and knowledge and share what you both know. Since you know these people so well and spend time around them, they are typically the ones from whom you pick up new habits. Recall that some of my writing habits were a result of spending extended periods of time with my dear friend Tammy. In a sense, this is the prototype relationship for the mentor-coach model, in which you work with people for a long time to get a deep sense of what they do and how they do it. Think back to the founding members in the chocolate-scented spray deodorant story. Because John, Harry, and Joan already knew each other well, it was easy for them to work together with ease and later reach out to Julie and her team.

Actions to take now to bring more value to close relationships with similar people

Begin these actions by taking a look at the three value questions and drilling down on them in two ways, asking, "Am I investing enough time in my relationships? And am I investing in the right relationships?"

Action 4.1 *Investing enough time in maintaining close relationships.* The capacity to build deep and enriching relationships is crucial to *Glow*. Here are three insights that might really make a difference:

These relationships are important to you, so they are worth investing in regular conversations.

Friendships deepen and become more valuable when you are both engaged in a similar task or activity. Make sure that you and your friends plan to spend time together engaged in common activities. For example, my friend Tammy and I always put aside at least a week every year for me to visit her on the farm, and during that time we always plan to write a short piece together. Without spending time together we could easily drift apart.

Rituals are wonderful ways of deepening friendships: the weekly lunch date, the monthly trip to the movies, brunch on Sundays—all are ways of strengthening the bonds of friendship.

Action 4.2   *Investing in the right relationships.* It is odd but often true that you can invest more time in antagonistic relationships that cause you grief than those that you find satisfying and rewarding. Are you investing too much time in unsatisfactory and conflicting relationships rather than in positive and life-enhancing ones? Here are three insights that might really make a difference:

- When you are with the other person, think about how you feel and whether you feel as if you are *Glowing*. If you do, this is a relationship worth investing in. If not, you have two options:

- If this is a relationship that is very precious to you but has gone sour, you may decide to keep on investing in the relationship while trying to shift it from unsatisfactory to satisfactory. Review Action 2, mastering the art of great conversation, particularly the portion on emotional conversations, and have a conversation about feelings.

- If this is a relationship that you have little hope for, now is the time to bring it to an end as decently as possible. Remember, you will never *Glow* if too much of your time is spent with people who drain your energy.

Quadrant 2: Close Friends Who Are Different from Me

History. These are people who are different from you and who over time have become close and precious. Like close friendships with people who are similar, these relationships are a valuable source of support and insight. The added bonus they bring is that since the person is different from you, his or her knowledge, insights, and habits can provide a valuable source of variety for you to expand on. Think back to our discussion of heuristics in Chapter Nine. Close friends who are similar to you are likely to have many overlapping heuristics because you have so much in common. Close friends who are different from you have fewer overlapping heuristics and hence more variety, and since you know and trust them, you are in a better position to learn from this variety rather than simply rejecting it.

Value. When you develop close relationships with people who are very different from you, it gives you a unique perspective on the world and provides the opportunity to explore and appreciate others' perspectives. Through this exploration, both of you are able to broaden your own understanding and increase your tolerance of variety and diversity. By developing close relationships with people who are different from you, you will become more tolerant, more open to differences, and therefore more skillful in the habit of cooperation.

☀ Actions to take now to bring more value to close relationships with people who are different from you

Again, begin these actions by taking a look at the three value questions and drilling down on them in two ways, asking, "Do I have a well-rounded network? And is there a balance in the length of time I have known people?"

Action 4.3   *Creating a well-rounded network.* It's easy when you are reaching out to people who are different from you to bias your relationships toward people in certain networks and positions. Here are three insights that might make a real difference in ensuring that you are reaching out to a wide range of people who are different from you.

- Reaching out to some people who have *higher status and power*— these can be valuable contacts when important decisions have to be made, resources have to be acquired, and political issues come into play.

- Reach out to *your colleagues and peers*—these can be valuable contacts for brainstorming and information sharing.

- Reach out to *younger, less skilled people*—these can be valuable contacts for mentoring and coaching.

Action 4.4   *Balancing familiarity.* Typically, you open up your networks with people who are different from you at certain times in your working life—perhaps when you first went to college or joined a company and met others during orientation or when you worked on a particular cross-business task. Take a look at the people in your network. Are the majority of them people you have known for a long time? If so, chances are that you have become more and more similar over time and are unlikely to hear new ideas and insights from them. Or are the majority of people in your network new friends? If this is the case, you could be lacking a sounding board and an empathic listener. Here are a couple of actions that could make a difference:

- Look at the names in Quadrant 2, and determine how long you have been friends with each of them. If they are all long-standing relationships, think about how you might open up your networks over the next year. Action 5, jumping out of the boundaries that constrain you, will show you how best to do this (see Chapter Eleven).

- If the relationships in Quadrant 2 are all relatively new, you may want to consider how to keep these relationships going over time. You may want to reflect on what it is you have done in the past that resulted in heritage relationships and lost contacts.

Close friends are crucial to your capacity to *Glow*. Acquaintances can also be valuable resources, since they require less intensive maintenance than close relationships, so you can have many more. In fact, you can have hundreds or even thousands. This "cloud of acquaintances," as I called it earlier, provides a huge potential pool of ideas and diversity. Are you making the most of your acquaintances?

Quadrant 3: Acquaintances Who Are Similar to Me

History. These are networks you have developed with people who are similar to you. When these relationships form a community of people who have similar interests, they are called *communities of practice,* in the sense that they have been built around common shared interests or experiences. These communities of practice can be marvelously exciting places that enhance your ability to *Glow.*

Value. These are great networks to help you learn more about the topics you are interested in. For example, I am a member of a network of people who are interested in positive psychology (you will find some of their works in the Recommended Reading section at the back of this book). This is an informal network of a couple of hundred of people around the world who communicate mostly through blogs, newsletters, and e-mail. Occasionally, we also meet to spend a couple of days together. This community is really important to me. I enjoy being part of it, and it is easy for me to interact with, since we all have the same interests and the same value sets. This conserves my emotional energy, in that I don't have to invest in finding and then learning to cooperate with people who are very different from me.

Communities of practice are a potentially important resource for you, and in Chapter Eleven you will have an opportunity to take a much closer look at how you can gain greater value from your current communities of practice and also reach out to other communities.

Quadrant 4: Acquaintances Who Are Different from Me

History. These are likely to be people you have met through a friend of a friend or you have bumped into. They form the networks you create when you are in *flâneur* mode, giving time to meeting people who are very different from you. They differ from relationships in Quadrant 3 in the sense that at the time of meeting, you probably did not have anything in common to bring you together.

Value. These relationships are created through classic jumping across worlds. Recall that in the example of the chocolates Orial and I designed, it was the combination of different ideas (chocolates and books) that was a real source of energy and innovation. The same was true for Harry and Julie—they *Glowed* because they had made an unusual combination (chocolate technology and spray deodorants). Each jumped across worlds—the chocolate maker and the writer, the taste specialist and the deodorant marketer. What's interesting about both these networks is that they had a strong unplanned, serendipitous aspect to them. I did not go out to find a chocolate maker, in the same way that Harry did not go out to find an expert in fragrances and essences.

There is a measure of serendipity in both cases—the unexpected, the unplanned, the random. That's why the metaphor about wandering around—becoming a *flâneur*—is such an important part of the creation of these networks. Take a look at Action 5, jumping out of the boundaries that constrain you, to see how you might get greater value from these types of networks (see Chapter Eleven).

Balance and Value

The networks that help you *Glow* and help you find, create, and flourish in Hot Spots have a balance between similarity and difference. When you become too embedded in relationships with people who you know very well, you leave little space in your working life for serendipity to open up the possibilities of meeting other people. And when you overemphasize similarity, you surround yourself with friends and acquaintances who have the same experiences and point of view as you have. This severely limits the heuristics at your disposal and will result in your becoming too narrow, less innovative, and ultimately less likely to *Glow.*

Key Points in Chapter Ten

ACTION 4

Increasing the Value of Your Networks

When you create valuable networks, you balance tight networks of acquaintances and friends who are similar to you with more extensive networks of people who are very different from you. Often the most stimulating and most innovative ideas come from people you barely know.

The most valuable strategy you can adopt to increase the value of your networks is to deepen your relationships with strong, trusting, and cooperative friends while also broadening your networks to encompass a wide variety of associates.

Your networks fall into four quadrants—close friends who are similar, close friends who are different, acquaintances and associates who are similar, and acquaintances and associates who are different .In this chapter we looked closely at the actions to take around two of these quadrants.

Close Friends Who Are Similar

These are people with whom you have a shared history, who can often be a source of energy in your life to help you *Glow*.

Action 4.1   Investing enough time in maintaining close relationships

Action 4.2   Investing in the right relationships

Close Friends Who Are Different

These people are a valuable source of support and insight, and since they are different from you, their knowledge, perceptions, and habits can broaden your perspectives and ideas.

Action 4.3   Creating a well-rounded network

Action 4.4   Balancing familiarity

The key is to create value by achieving a balance between closeness and distance and between similarity and difference.

Chapter Eleven

ACTION 5

Jumping out of the Boundaries That Constrain You

People who Glow have broad and extensive networks and are skilled at jumping out of the boundaries that constrain them. They allow for serendipity in their life and are prepared to meet new people and take the untrodden path to broaden their experiences.

When you create extensive and meandering networks, you *Glow*, as these networks ensure that you create, find and flourish in Hot Spots.

You have two diagnostics to help you understand whether this is an action you should be focusing on. The first is your responses in the *Glow* Profile in Figure 8.1. This will give you a good idea of how adept you are at jumping across worlds. If your final profile is Profile Type D or E, this action is particularly crucial to you. Also take a look at the names you wrote in the four quadrants in Figure 10.1. Are the relationships in Quadrants 3 and 4 taking as much time as those in Quadrants 1 and 2? Are they as well developed? If you are spending too much time walking the same patch with the same people, Action 5 is crucial for you.

In this chapter you will take a closer look at Quadrants 3 and 4. Our discussion of Quadrant 3 will focus on how to build more valuable communities of practice so that you can broaden your networks with people who are similar to you and therefore gain more value from rapid knowledge flows. Our discussion of Quadrant 4 will explain how to create more value by becoming a *flâneur* so that you can enter into the lives of others with passion and interest and thereby gain more innovative value through combining different ideas.

Quadrant 3: How to Build More Valuable Communities of Practice

You can begin by reviewing your responses in Quadrant 3 in Figure 10.1. In that quadrant you named three people representative of acquaintances and associates who are similar to you.

Typically, your communities of practice develop through a combination of three factors:

- They are people who share a problem that they all believe to be important (for example, how can we make this company more carbon-neutral?).

- They are people who have a shared passion for a topic (for example, increasing the number of computers in African villages).

- They are people who seek to deepen and extend their knowledge by getting together on a regular basis (for example, to learn more about how change takes place in an organization or to talk about a book they have all read).

Communities of practice that can develop great value don't all have to be about earth-shattering topics. Even the most seemingly mundane day-to-day issue can spark a valuable community of practice. Take the example of my friend Marilyn, who is a great networker. She tells me that the most active community she is a member of is a community dedicated to helping people housebreak cats. It is full of people blogging about their cat problems, videos of how they resolved them, people volunteering to mentor others—and all completely virtual: none of the members of the community have ever met.

As Marilyn's example shows, you have to be interested in something and be prepared to give time to it for a community of practice to emerge. As the community develops and you connect more with each other, you begin to share more information, insights, and advice. Your communities of practice help you solve the problems you face; they can discuss the situations that are worrying you and explore ideas that interest you. What a community of practice is great at is creating potential value for you to become more innovative and more able to *Glow*.

Your communities of practice come in all shapes and sizes. They can be small and intimate, involving only a few people, or large, with many members and subdivisions. They can be short-lived or flourish over decades. They can be made up of people who have much in common or who have less in common except for a single passion. They can be based in a single business unit, range across a whole company, or transcend organizational boundaries to connect people from many organizations. The members of your community of practice can be colocated, so that you bump into each other naturally as the day unfolds, or virtual, distributed across a country or indeed the globe, so that you rely on e-mail, blogging, and perhaps the occasional meeting to keep the connections alive. Your communities of practice can arise spontaneously, without your intervention or development effort, or they can be intentionally formed by calling meetings, setting agendas, and creating supporting tools such as Web sites or knowledge bases.

Reviewing Your Communities of Practice

It's a good idea to review your communities of practice on a regular basis to decide whether you should be changing your role in the communities you are in or perhaps even reaching out to other communities.

Increasing the value of your current communities of practice

To review your communities, first take a moment to think about the communities of practice you are currently a member of. Use the following descriptions to categorize the communities:

- Communities that are about a challenge I face at work
- Communities that focus on something I am passionate about
- Communities that meet to share ideas
- Communities that are outside of work

Next, think about each of these communities and the impact your membership is having on your feeling of well-being and your capacity to *Glow*.

Finally, for each community of practice, ask yourself these three questions:

- Am I investing the right amount of time in these communities of practice? (Actions 5.1 and 5.2 may help you decide on this.)
- Are my communities of practice providing me with the breadth of networks I need to find and create Hot Spots that enable me to Glow? (Actions 5.3, 5.4, and 5.5 may help you widen your networks.)
- Are there areas of emerging interest in my life for which I have not yet developed a community? (Here too, Actions 5.3, 5.4, and 5.5 may help.)

Your answers to these questions will help you decide which actions you should take now to ensure you have the right communities of practice to deliver value.

Actions to take now to create valuable communities of practice

Action 5.1 *Optimizing the time spent in communities of practice.* First, think about the amount of time you spend in each of the communities of practice, and consider whether this amount of time is optimal for creating value. There are potentially three broad levels of involvement:

- At the highest level of involvement, you are currently interacting intensively and participate a great deal in shaping the community. The question to reflect on is, "Should I be standing back a little more?"

- At the next level of involvement, you are currently an active member of this community and make a regular contribution. The question you should reflect on is, "Should I be increasing or decreasing my participation?"

- At the lowest level of involvement, you are currently staying on the periphery and rarely participate actively. The question to reflect on is, "Should I be putting more energy into this community?"

Action 5.2 *Creating value in communities of practice.* Reflecting further on the amount of time you are spending in each community, evaluate how valuable the community has been for you.

Consider whether you need to shift roles among the three levels of involvement, perhaps becoming more central to the community or disengaging from the everyday flow of the community and moving out to a more peripheral membership.

You don't need to be in the center to gain value from a community of practice. In fact, being on the sidelines and connecting through associates can let you gain insight and watch what is going on without making a major commitment of time or resources.

Remember that you have finite resources available to build and develop your network of friends and associates, so if you want to extend your communities of practice, it may be wise to move to a more peripheral role.

Quadrant 4: How to Create Value as a Flâneur

Think back to Quadrant 4 in Figure 8.1 and the extent to which these networks allow for the possibility of serendipity in your life. It is often from these unexpected connections that innovation emerges.

You can create these unexpected encounters by becoming a *flâneur*, being prepared to wander around with no fixed idea of where you are going.

Be interested and inquisitive about what you see and positive and open to the people you meet.

When you become a *flâneur*, you bring flux and transformation, fleeting relations and connections into your networks. In your wanderings you rediscover acquaintances you carry in your memory rather than through regular interaction. You encounter strangers, some of whom you will meet again. It is in these fleeting encounters that you gossip, exchange unexpected news and details, develop new perspectives, and glean new insights.

Becoming a *flâneur* is both an attitude of mind and a decision to give time to serendipity. It can also be encouraged by your physical space. Some places are built for the *flâneur*. Thinking back to my own chocolate story, the Mediterranean town in which I live is tailor-made for the *flâneur*. The climate is mild; the streets are so narrow that you are forced to bump into people; there are no cars, so there is no danger as you wander; and the outdoor cafés and tapas bars encourage waving, stopping, and chatting. It is easy to become a *flâneur* in this town, to wander where you please with no fixed plan or predetermined destination, to devote time to the activity and keep an open mind to appreciate all you see.

However, you don't have to be in a Mediterranean town to become a *flâneur*. Remember how Harry and Julie met. They were not strolling around a quaint village. But they were taking time out to participate in an executive program. When not in lectures, they spent time talking with each other over coffee, and after the conference, devoted even more time to catching up and talking more. If you want to be a great *flâneur*, even in a cold northern climate, you need to adopt and pursue four precepts:

- Allow for serendipity in your working life; do not overschedule your time to the point that any possibility of the unexpected is excluded.

- Use the unscheduled time to go off the beaten path.

- Be positive and warm to the strangers you encounter.

- Cultivate a fluid identity that ensures you will be welcomed as you jump across worlds.

Allowing for Serendipity in Your Life

Tight schedules can eliminate any possibility of wandering around, so the first action to take is to schedule time for the unexpected and then just let the moment take you. Here are three actions that you can take right now:

☀ *Actions to take now to allow for serendipity in your life*

Action 5.3 *Setting aside "golden moments."* This is a little trick I play on myself to encourage me to leave some time unscheduled. Every couple of months, I take a pen with gold ink (the gold ink seems to be more difficult to cross out later) and go through my desk calendar, blocking out time every week to wander around and let serendipity into my working life. Some weeks it's a couple of hours; other weeks it could be a day or two. So buy yourself a gold pen and get that calendar out! I am aware that this is easier for me because as an academic I have freedom built into my worklife. But even if you are in a highly scheduled job it is crucial that you allow yourself time out to wander and reflect. In the short term this may seem counterproductive, in the longer term it will help you be more innovative and creative.

Action 5.4 *Taking time out.* Encourage your team members and manager to give you time to work on something that is different from your day-to-day work and enables you to meet with different people. You might point out to them that at Google, employees are allowed 10 percent of their time to work on something of their own.

Action 5.5 *Taking minisabbaticals.* You can expect your working life between now and the time you retire to be more of a "portfolio" than a direct, hierarchical line to the top. Part of the portfolio will be opportunities for you to take time off for personal development. So when you take this time off, recognize that these are great opportunities for you to release your inner *flâneur* by developing a new skill, traveling to another city, state, or country, or jumping into a completely different situation.

Going off the Beaten Path

Be sure that in the time you have carved out in your working life, you are really engaging in jumping across worlds. The emphasis here is on creating broader networks with people who are different from you.

☀ *Actions to take now to create broader networks*

Action 5.6 *Creating broader networks.* Make sure you engage with different people in your normal day-to-day activities. For example, when you play tennis, chess, or computer games, play each game with different people. In Action 6, finding and moving to boundaryless places (Chapter Twelve), you will get an opportunity to look at this in more detail; here is a summary of the ideas you will encounter there:

- Pursue a career path in which you are able to move across functions, businesses or countries.

- Seek out mentors with wide, diverse networks.

- Make it known that you want to work in different functions or businesses.

- Attend seminars and meetings outside your own group.

- Join communities of practice outside your immediate work group.

- Volunteer for socially responsible projects.

- Widen your social and sports activities.

Being Positive and Warm to the Strangers You Encounter

Expert *flâneurs* gain from their wanderings because when they meet strangers, they are good-mannered and courteous. The philosopher Bertrand Russell summed up this state of mind perfectly in *The Conquest of Happiness:*

> *Fundamental happiness depends more than anything else upon what may be called a friendly interest in persons and things.*

A friendly interest in persons is a form of affectionateness, but not the form which is grasping and possessive and seeking always an emphatic response. This latter form is very frequently a source of unhappiness. The kind that makes for happiness is the kind that likes to observe people and finds pleasure in their individual traits, that wishes to afford scope for the interests and pleasures of those with whom it is brought into contact without desiring to acquire power over them or to secure their enthusiastic admiration. The person whose attitude towards others is genuinely of this kind will be a source of happiness and a recipient of reciprocal kindness.

Actions to take now to become more positive and warm with strangers

Action 5.7   *Showing interest in others and appreciating others.* Ensure that you are mentally and physically engaged in conversations and meetings, showing your interest in others. Be curious about the world around you. Learn to appreciate people who are different from you, find out what they do, why they do it, and how they developed these habits and skills.

Cultivating a Fluid Identity

On the face of it, jumping across worlds sounds easy. However, one of the reasons you do it perhaps less than you might is that in reality it is far from easy. Take Harry and Julie, for example. Although they have a lot in common, in reality they inhabit different worlds of work. Julie is on the essence and fragrance team that worked on Magnum ice cream. Most members of her team have a research background and postgraduate qualifications. If you observed one of her team meetings, you would hear people deep in technical conversation. They would be discussing the complexities of keeping these essences and fragrances stable and how the substances behave under pressure and at low temperatures. Julie and her team use a language dominated by technical and mathematical terms and are relaxed about long, unstructured meetings.

Now let's observe Harry and his team. Many members of his team are from a production or marketing background, and their meetings tend to be decisive, short-term oriented, and pragmatic.

Both teams have developed their own norms and ways of behaving. For example, how you dress (Julie's team: jeans and T-shirt; Harry's team: business suit), when you turn up for meetings (Julie's team: fifteen minutes late is fine; Harry's team: punctuality is demanded), and what you talk about (Julie's team: long conversations about molecular formation; Harry's team: short-term marketing problems).

See the challenge? When Julie meets Harry, they are not just jumping beyond their team; they are actually connecting to a world very different from their own.

If you want to be adept at jumping across worlds, you have to develop a fluid identity. What that involves is taking some of the norms from the other world while remaining authentic to yourself. Julie has something of a fluid identity. For example, when she is in Harry's world, Julie does not use the technical jargon that is common parlance in her own team; she also dresses in a more formal way and makes sure that she comes to meetings at the appointed time. She is able to sound "research" when with her own group and "marketing" when in Harry's world.

Do you want to develop a more fluid identity? You can take action right now.

Actions to take now that will help you develop a fluid identity

Action 5.8 *Developing a fluid identity.* It will help greatly if you can become more aware of yourself and the norms of your own team and community so that you recognize the differences between your own world and others' worlds. There are two ways to do this:

- *Become extrasensitive to the norms of others,* how others behave, the language they use, and their attitudes toward time. Julie quickly learned that some of the R&D jargon she used with her own team was not going to be meaningful in Harry's world, so she modified her use of jargon and learned some key marketing terms.

■ *Monitor the impact you are having on others.* Watching other people's reactions to you will help you become more aware of their norms and the norms you may be violating. For example, Julie modified her technical language because she saw how Harry's team responded to her initially. She also noticed the subtle reactions when she was a few minutes late, even though nobody said anything. By monitoring her effect on others, she could figure out what to change. In a sense, she was able to become a "social chameleon," adept at adapting to different situations.

Having a more fluid identity does not mean that you lose your authentic self. In Julie's case, there are aspects of her behavior and values that she is not prepared to compromise on. A good example of this is the handling of deadlines. When she is with Harry's team, she is not prepared to agree to the shortened deadlines that Harry's team always seems to want. The norm in Harry's team is that everything should be done "yesterday" or "as soon as possible." But she knows that the members of her team hate working under what they consider unreasonable pressure. So while she compromises on the clothes she wears and the language she uses, she does not compromise on the time she needs to work through a problem.

Key Points in Chapter Eleven

Action 5

Jumping out of the Boundaries That Constrain You

It is wise to become skilled at escaping the boundaries that constrain you by building more valuable communities of practice and creating value as a *flâneur*—being prepared to wander away from your natural networks.

Building More Valuable Communities of Practice
Communities of practice consist of people who share a problem, a passion, or an interest in deepening an area of knowledge. The emphasis is on increasing the value of communities of practice by investing the right amount of time, ensuring that they create a broad network, and picking up on emerging interests.

Action 5.1 Optimizing the time spent in communities of practice

Action 5.2 Creating value in communities of practice

Creating Value as a Flâneur
As you wander outside your normal networks, you must be interested and inquisitive about what you see and positive and open about the people you meet. To do this, you need to allow for serendipity in your life.

Action 5.3 Setting aside "golden moments"

Action 5.4 Taking time out

Action 5.5 Taking minisabbaticals

Action 5.6 Creating broader networks

Action 5.7 Showing interest in others and appreciating others

Action 5.8 Developing a fluid identity

Chapter Twelve

ACTION 6

Finding and Moving to Boundaryless Places

People who Glow are adept at finding and moving to boundaryless places. They know how to escape from the Fortress and connect with teams and places that encourage them to grow by creating opportunities to jump across worlds.

Look back at your profile in Figure 8.1. If yours is Profile Type C, D, or E, you are currently with a team or a company that does not encourage you to jump across worlds—in fact, you could even be holed up in a Fortress with high walls around you. The ability to *Glow* is within you, of course, but it is also dependent on the context you are in—the friends and networks you have and the community, organization, or business you are working in.

Recall that in Action 3 you reflected on what it is like to be in a place where there is little cooperation and considered what it would take to become skilled at understanding and acting on the "smell of the place." The same is true of jumping across worlds. If there are big walls around you, you may find it mighty hard to scale them; you feel as if you are trapped in a Fortress. So this chapter is about how in the short term to really make the best of where you are now while also in the longer term learning to spot and then join places that are boundaryless.

In the Short Term: Making the Most of Jumping Across Worlds

You will be surprised at how much potential there is to jump across worlds— even in a high-walled Fortress. Here are seven actions you can take right now to make the most of your current opportunities.

☼ Actions to take now to jump across your current boundaries

Action 6.1 *Pursue a boundary-crossing career path.* Careers come in two shapes. There are highly specialized jobs where you need to focus on competence and knowledge in a single tightly defined area; typically, these careers provide you with very little opportunity to cross boundaries. There are other career paths that encourage you to move across disciplines or functions. If you want to have the opportunity to jump across worlds, take the career path that has cross-boundary work built into it.

Action 6.2 *Seek out mentors with wide, diverse networks.* One of the best ways to create opportunities to jump across worlds is to align yourself with a mentor who has a wide network and who is prepared to share these connections with you and encourage you to jump across the different worlds the mentor has networks in.

Action 6.3 *Make it known that you want to work in different functions or businesses.* You will be surprised how many opportunities there are for you to join projects and task forces that cross boundaries. So find out what these are, and make it known that you want to broaden your experience by participating in them.

Action 6.4 *Attend seminars and meetings outside your own group.* A great way to jump across worlds is to find out how people who are different from you go about sharing knowledge. It could be that they meet at seminars or brown-bag lunches. Just by showing your face, you are more likely to be invited to participate in a shared activity with them.

Action 6.5 *Join communities of practice outside your immediate work group.* Think back to communities of practice you considered in Action 5 (Chapter Eleven), and identify a couple that you are interested in outside your normal network.

Action 6.6 *Volunteer for socially responsible projects.* A quick and relatively easy way to jump across worlds is to volunteer to join projects and task forces in the community. Inevitably, these will involve people from different worlds and can provide a great opportunity for you to broaden your networks.

Action 6.7 *Widen your social and sports activities.* Another way of escaping a Fortress is to join social and sporting activities where the participants are drawn from a much wider community.

So there is much you can do right now—even if you are in a Fortress—to experience jumping across worlds. However, no matter how successfully you manage to push back the boundaries, over time it could well be that the walls will close in on you and reduce your capacity to *Glow.* So next time you decide on a job move, the opportunity to jump across worlds should be high on your list of selection criteria. You should be on the lookout for a team, business, or company that is boundaryless.

How are you going to do this? Think back to Action 3, acting on the "smell of the place," explored in Chapter Seven. You will need the same sort of detective skills and a cool-headed, analytical, rational view of what the company has to offer. Here is how you can do this.

In the Longer Term: Moving to Boundaryless Places

You want to be sure that your next job choice is more informed. Like many of us, you have probably in the past joined a company or accepted a project on the basis of rather superficial information. Perhaps you just accepted the first offer. So you may have fallen into a job that looked deceptively attractive but turned out to be a Fortress that depleted rather than replenished your resources.

To avoid joining a Fortress again, you need to understand what is really going on in the company. Remember that most companies are adept at sales pitches; they have marketing gurus and brand experts whose job it is to tell you what they want you to know, and they may not advertise the sort of information you need. So be prepared to go beneath the surface of the glossy ads and the marketing spiel. Seek answers to the question "Will this place encourage me to jump across worlds?"

If you want to do some detective work on the company before you decide whether to join it, you will have to do some digging. Here are three strategies you can adopt, followed by five questions to ask.

☀ Actions to take now to broaden your sources of information

Action 6.8   *Ask tough questions in the interview.* When you are being interviewed for a job, make sure that near the end of the session you ask about potential career paths. That way you can glimpse whether people stay within their own boundaries of functions or businesses or whether they have opportunities to cross boundaries.

Action 6.9   *Examine the career information.* Look at whatever career information is available to see how the career paths of current employees have typically developed. What you are looking for here is that people have had the opportunity to move around.

Action 6.10   *Seek feedback from friends or online.* Use your networks to locate people who have worked or are working at the company, and ask their opinions. Alumni networks are often good places to begin. Or search online: current and past employees are posting more and more information about their experiences of working for various companies.

To give you more insight about this I have created five multiple-choice questions which provide more detailed information about the broad themes.

These questions will help you discover whether the company is a Fortress or a place where boundaries are crossed and different worlds meet. The response options are arranged from most encouraging of jumping across worlds (a) to least encouraging (c).

1. What is the typical career path of executives in this company?

If you want to know whether the company encourages the crossing of boundaries, start with the career path of the person you are talking with. It is likely that your interviewer's experience will be reflective of what is valued in the company as a whole.

a. Many executives have experience working in different sectors and businesses.

b. Most of the executives spend their career with the company, although they do get an opportunity to work across a number of different businesses and functions.

c. The executive has stayed in one function or business.

2. What development opportunities are provided for high-potential employees?

One of the great ways of becoming adept at jumping across worlds is to have career opportunities that allow you to participate in various functions and businesses of the company. Beware of companies where the emphasis is on people staying within their own specialized areas without ever collaborating with people in other disciplines.

a. There are a number of career practices that ensure people have the opportunity to work in many different functions and businesses of the company and to connect to people in other companies and communities.

b. The career path ensures that you stay in the sector but work in different businesses.

c. People typically stay in the same business or function.

3. How are job openings filled?

You are more likely to jump across worlds if you have an idea of what is going on in other parts of the business. If most of the selection decisions are made behind closed doors, it will be difficult for you to get sufficient information about what is available. It is better to join a company where all the jobs are posted so that you can apply for jobs outside your own part of the business.

a. There is an open job-posting system in which all the jobs are advertised and anyone can be considered, regardless of the business in which they are currently located.

b. There is an open job-posting system in which you may apply for a job if you are already employed in that business or function.

c. Job vacancies are not advertised, and most placement decisions are made by senior executives.

4. How are projects and task forces staffed?

Working on projects and task forces that are outside your current area of expertise is a great way to develop your capabilities to cross boundaries and increase the span of your network. Again, what you are looking for is the opportunity to put your hand up when projects come up. If projects are always filled with people in the "old boys' network," you are unlikely to have a shot at them.

a. Project and task force opportunities are advertised, and anyone can apply and be considered.

b. Project and task force opportunities are decided by executives who look for candidates across all businesses and functions.

c. Project and task force opportunities are decided by executives, and participants are chosen from within the business or function.

5. What opportunities are there to get involved with communities outside the immediate work?

Joining other groups and volunteering for communities of practice can play a crucial role in enabling and supporting you to jump across worlds. If you are in a company that encourages employees to join clubs and networks, this can significantly increase your capabilities.

    a. People are actively encouraged to become involved in activities outside their immediate work.

    b. People are allowed to become involved in activities outside their immediate work.

    c. People are discouraged from becoming involved in activities outside their immediate work.

Scoring is simple. If your answers are mostly a's, this is a boundaryless place; jump at the opportunity to join. If mostly b's, there will be opportunities for you to jump across worlds; just make sure you take them. If mostly c's, this is a Fortress; it's unlikely to be a place in which you can *Glow*, so don't get locked inside.

Key Points in Chapter Twelve

ACTION 6

Finding and Moving to Boundaryless Places

It is important that you become adept at moving to boundaryless places and avoiding the traps of the Fortress. Instead find places where you can cross boundaries and jump across worlds. You can do this in the shorter term by making the best of where you are and in the longer term by learning to identify and then join places that are boundaryless.

Making the Most of Jumping Across Worlds

There is potential to create broader networks in even the highest-walled Fortress.

Action 6.1   Pursuing a boundary-crossing career path

Action 6.2   Seeking out mentors with wide, diverse networks

Action 6.3   Making it known that you want to work in different functions or businesses

Action 6.4   Attending seminars and meetings outside your own group

Action 6.5   Joining communities of practice outside your immediate work group

Action 6.6   Volunteering for socially responsible projects

Action 6.7   Widening your social and sports activities

Moving to Boundaryless Places

You want to make sure that your next job move is more informed, and to do this you need to create a real understanding of the company or the community before you join it. Gather information about the company by taking these actions and asking tough questions.

Action 6.8   Asking tough questions in the interview

Action 6.9   Examining the career information

Action 6.10   Seeking feedback from friends or online

Chapter Thirteen

The Third Principle: Igniting Latent Energy

You've created latent energy by behaving in a cooperative way and by jumping across worlds; now the scene is set for ignition. Without these sparks of ignition, you are consigning yourself to a Country Club, a place where you feel comfortable and at ease but in which you will never, ever *Glow*.

This is the third principle of *Glowing*. First you will hear one man's story of how he created enormous energy and innovation throughout a whole community of people and became a superb catalyst to help everyone *Glow*. Then you will complete the *Glow* Profile to identify your specific profile type before looking at the three actions that can ignite you:

Action 7 *Asking the questions that spark energy* and also have the capacity to ignite and excite others.

Action 8 *Creating a vision that compels* others and demonstrates your beliefs and passion.

Action 9 *Crafting meaningful and exciting work* that provides you and your colleagues with an opportunity to stretch your capabilities, develop new skills, and ultimately *Glow*.

When I asked people who *Glow* what it mean to ignite the energy around them, this is how they described their experiences:

> *"I felt as if the whole place was buzzing. We all knew that this was an important question that was meaningful to each one of us."*

> *"What was great was the opportunity to talk about something that came from my heart. I had an opportunity to talk about a vision I really believed in."*

> *"I knew I was Glowing because people could see how involved and excited I was."*

> *"I had inherited a really dreary job, but I managed to turn it around and make it into something that made me pleased to wake up in the morning."*

> *"After years of sitting quietly, I finally had the courage to ask the questions that I felt were critical—and I was amazed at how appreciative people were."*

> *"I am proud that my colleagues and I crafted a task that sparked energy in lots of people and drew people toward it."*

> *"I feel really inspired by what I am doing—and I know that people can see my inspiration."*

Think about your own experiences of *Glowing*. Have there been times when you also felt this level of excitement and involvement?

Contrast this with how people described being in a situation when their energy had not been ignited:

> *"I felt content but incredibly bored."*

> *"Sometimes I found myself almost asleep at my desk. I struggled to get through the day."*

> *"What was really disappointing is that I never felt that I had brought my real self to work; I never felt truly engaged."*

> *"It was one of those places where you never dared question anything. The most important thing was to keep your head down."*

"Everything was so short-term. We never sat back for a moment and decided what we wanted to do or be in the long term. It was like living in that movie Groundhog Day—every day was the same!"

"I never really got the point of what I was doing. I couldn't make a connection between myself and my work."

Country Clubs come in different shapes and sizes, but what they have in common is that they dislocate you from your work. This means that you never really get an opportunity to put your true self into your work. The challenge is that when you lose your true self at work, you no longer *Glow*. All of us one time or another have found ourselves in a place where there is little energy. But if you want to *Glow*, you have to reconnect with your imagination, your passion, and your energy.

In this chapter you will learn how to find your true self and express your energy and excitement through the questions you ask, the vision for the future you create, and the jobs that you do. Let me illustrate this with the story of a man who *Glows* brightly and through his beliefs and passions created Hot Spots throughout a community.

When Sparks Fly: The One-Lakh Car

I had arrived in India in time for a great celebration in the business community. Just that week, one of India's preeminent car manufacturers, the Tata Group, had launched a new car called the Nano at the New Delhi Motor Show. Many new models from American, European, and Asian car manufacturers had been launched at the show, but it was the Nano that captured the imagination of the crowd and the press. The papers were full of pictures and stories about the car, and in every party I went to (all part of the role of a *flâneur*), it had been the center of conversation. It was quite literally the talk of the town. Why all the fuss about a car?

This is how company chairman Ratan Tata had introduced the car at the New Delhi show. Against a hologram of a typical Indian family of four wobbling on a motorbike, in a quiet, dignified voice, Tata had this to say:

> *I observed families riding on two-wheelers—the father driving the scooter, his child standing in front of him, his wife seated behind holding a baby. It led me to wonder whether one could conceive of a safe, affordable, all-weather form of transport for such a family. Tata Motor's engineers and designers gave their all for about four years to realize this goal. Today we indeed have a people's car that is affordable and yet built to meet safety requirements and emission norms, to be fuel-efficient and yet low on emissions.*

Anyone who has been to India cannot help but be struck by the ingenuity with which people and goods are transported on two wheels. Whole families on scooters are commonplace—I have also seen small calves transported in this way. The case for the Nano is clear. What Tata had created was a Hot Spot in which excitement, passion, and creativity poured into the design of a car and provided everyone involved in its creation with a marvelous opportunity to *Glow*.

What sparked all this energy was the passion and belief of one man, Ratan Tata. Now in his seventies, Tata is one of the most revered India business leaders of his time. He leads a fifth-generation business that has grown to become one of the world's most admired philanthropic companies, joining other dynasties such as the Mellon family as recipients of the Carnegie Medal of Philanthropy. The Tatas are devout Parsis, and the company is a strong proponent of corporate social responsibility, giving between 8 and 14 percent of its net profits to literacy, microfinancing, and water conservation projects across India.

What Tata did—and I have seen others who *Glow* do the same—was reach inside of himself to an issue or a theme that he feels passionate about. Of course, to do so he needs to really understand himself, know what he is passionate about, and have the courage to speak out—themes you will be returning to in Action 7, asking questions that spark energy, in Chapter

Fourteen. What Ratan Tata did was not only inspire himself to *Glow* but also ignite the passion of thousands of employees in the Tata Group. The question Tata had the courage to ask himself and everyone else in the company was deceptively simple: "Why can't we build a one-lakh car?"

A lakh is 100,000 rupees, equivalent to about $2,000. So asking for a car that sells for only $2,000 seems like a pretty sparky question by any account. Action 7 provides a number of tools and techniques that will help you develop questions that could have the same sparky resonance as this one.

Ratan Tata knew he was asking a lot when he raised the question about a car that retails for such a low price. But he also knew that in a country of over a billion people, many of whom have limited access to personal transport beyond a bicycle or a scooter, it was a vital question. He had seen and heard of too many people killed on India's treacherous roads to let the question go unanswered.

The courageous question he asked sparked energy throughout the company, and in early 2008, Tata was able to unveil the one-lakh car. Imagine how it felt for the people who engineered the car—you can imagine they were positively *Glowing*. When I spoke to the engineers about their feat, their sense of pride was palpable. As one of the engineers told me:

> *It seemed like an absolutely impossible question. No one could believe we could do it. There was a lot of cynicism—people thought we would just make two motorcycles joined at the hip or a supercharged auto-rickshaw. But we were determined to do it. It meant going back to basics, reengineering many of the parts, working closely with our component suppliers such as Bosch, and fundamentally questioning the way we do everything.*

Sure, what they produced was simple engineering, and as one correspondent ruefully observed at the time, "The average wristwatch has more instrumentation." Nevertheless, the engineering and production feat was extraordinary.

Clearly, if you want to *Glow*, you have to find something in your daily work that excites and intrigues you and has the possibility of sparking the energy of others.

How are you going to do this? I have found that there are three ways that you can ignite the energy inside of you and others.

Questions That Spark Energy

You can ignite your own energy and that of others by asking a question that really sets the place on fire. That's what Ratan Tata did when he asked the question "Why can't we make a one-lakh car?" What was audacious and courageous about this question was that he did not raise the question of simply shaving 20 percent off the cost of a car. His question focused on the very basis of what a car costs.

Asking this sort of audacious question can be crucial to feeling truly alive—to *Glowing*. In our discussion of Action 7 in Chapter Fourteen, you will hear about how Johanna created enormous energy by asking a string of audacious questions and also discover the four ways you can become skilled at developing and asking questions that ignite.

Visions That Compel

Questions are a marvelous way of generating the sparks that make you *Glow*. Sometimes the basis of these questions is an idea or a vision you have about something or yourself. This was certainly the case for Ratan Tata, the latest member of a family with a long history of participating in the wider Indian community and a vision of alleviating poverty in Indian society. So when Tata asked the "one-lakh" question, he was envisioning a way his company could contribute to society. Visions typically begin with the words "Imagine a world where . . . ." Tata's vision was this: "Imagine a world where rural communities can access the transport infrastructure so crucial for their development." He understood that getting their produce to market as quickly as possible would transform the lives of the farming community in rural India. Too often in his trips around the country he had seen fruit and vegetables rotting in the fields because villagers did not have speedy transportation to local and regional markets. Imagine how life would change if the rural population of India had access to local, regional, and world markets!

To truly *Glow,* you need to access your innermost passions and beliefs about the world and about how you and others can work together. In our discussion of Action 8, creating visions that compel, in Chapter Fifteen, you will discover how you can craft a vision for yourself and others that feels truly inspiring and helps you *Glow.*

Work That Is Meaningful and Exciting

You *Glow* when there is something in your life that excites and interests you. It could be the possibility of answering a question that fills you with interest or pursuing a vision that engages and excites you. But what of your day-to-day work? How are you going to *Glow* on your job every day?

You can find an answer in the Nano story. Beyond the questions and the vision is the day-to-day reality of working on a series of igniting tasks. These tasks could be as specific as rewriting the owner's manual or working with suppliers to reengineer a particular part or redesigning the interior. The creation of the Nano car was the result of countless smaller igniting tasks.

In our discussion of Action 9, crafting meaningful and exciting work, in Chapter Sixteen, you get to take a close look at your current job and decide what you might do to create opportunities to become engaged in more exciting and more stimulating work.

Beware the Country Club

It was the combination of a vision (bringing commerce to rural India), an audacious question ("Why can't we create the one-lakh car?"), and a complex task (reconceptualizing a vehicle in its entirety) that together ignited a Hot Spot of energy and innovation that burned bright at Tata for more than four years and caused everyone who worked on the project to *Glow.*

Igniting latent energy unleashes the engagement and excitement of *Glowing* and the marvelous experience of being in a Hot Spot. Without that igniting spark, what you get instead is a Country Club. If people are cooperating nicely, you have the satisfaction of being surrounded by well-wishers. But if there is no spark to ignite the latent energy in yourself and others, you fail to *Glow,* and high-energy Hot Spots fail to develop. The potential energy remains untapped, fading away in a mundane environment.

Places matter. The Big Freeze—the antithesis of working cooperatively together—is easy to spot. It's clear that people don't get along. The atmosphere crackles with politics and ill will. The same is true where people fail to jump across worlds—in the resulting Fortress, the walls people and teams are building around themselves are almost palpable. Country Clubs are more difficult to spot, even though they can snuff out the possibility of *Glowing* with as much force as the Big Freeze. They just arise in a more insidious and less transparent manner.

Chances are that you have been in a Country Club at some time in your working life. It's a place where everyone seems content and even happy, and you might infer that these are places where you are likely to *Glow.* But they are not. In the Country Club, underperformance is the norm, energy rarely sizzles, and the mundane is venerated. In the Country Club, the big questions are stifled, visions are uninspired, and tasks are overspecified and homogenized.

So beware the trap of the Country Club. Here are the five telltale signs of a Country Club:

- *Conflict seems remarkably low;* everyone seems to agree with everyone else. There are none of the sparks of conflict that can ignite energy. "Never is heard a discouraging word."

- *Complacency is the norm*—there is an unquestioning belief in the status quo and an assumption that everything will continue as it has in the past.

- *People are busy;* but be aware that busyness can mask a lack of focus and avoidance of the big questions.

- *You sense that there are important matters that are being ignored.* But if you question why things are done in a certain way, you are made to feel that you don't really understand or that you are somehow naïve.

- *You notice that everyone is rather similar.* They look about the same, they act the same, and they have the same point of view. Conformity is the norm. It is the corporate equivalent of the Stepford Wives.

These are rather subtle signs—you may have to behave a little like a social anthropologist to pick up on them. But you can. Just observe carefully, look for hidden signs, listen quietly, and take account of underlying trends. If you spot these signs, now is the time to take action, before you abandon any hope of *Glowing*.

The Glow Profile

Figure 13.1, together with the actions discussed in Chapters Fourteen, Fifteen, and Sixteen, will give you concrete and useful ways to tackle the Country Club problem. You must recognize that the Country Club is a trap; you have to make sure you don't fall into one, or if by chance you do, make sure you get out as quickly as possible before you forfeit your chance to *Glow*.

Profiling the Third Principle: Igniting Latent Energy

Do you, your immediate team, and your wider community, business, or organization promote the igniting of latent energy? The rating scales in Figure 13.1 will help you find out.

Respond to each statement by circling your reaction on the 5-point scale, as follows:

5 = agree completely

4 = agree somewhat

3 = neither agree nor disagree

2 = disagree somewhat

1 = disagree completely

Do I naturally ignite latent energy?

- I am always asking questions and am curious about how things are done. 5 4 3 2 1
- People describe me as naturally interested in what's happening around me. 5 4 3 2 1
- I have ideas about my work that I think are really important. 5 4 3 2 1
- I try to read as widely as possible to see what is going on outside my job. 5 4 3 2 1
- There are disciplines outside of my job that I find really fascinating. 5 4 3 2 1
- It is important to me to know that my ideas are fresh and exciting. 5 4 3 2 1
- I seem to have a natural skill for exciting others about ideas. 5 4 3 2 1
- It is important to me to leave time aside each week to think and talk about ideas unrelated to my work. 5 4 3 2 1
- I really enjoy creating work that is exciting and interesting for others. 5 4 3 2 1

Does my team naturally ignite latent energy?

- On this team, we often question each other about what we are doing. 5 4 3 2 1
- It is not unusual for people on this team to come up with ideas that others find exciting and interesting. 5 4 3 2 1
- We take time to talk to each other about ideas that excite us. 5 4 3 2 1
- We often invite different types of people to come in and talk with us. 5 4 3 2 1
- It is accepted that that we talk about the future and what we believe will be happening in the future. 5 4 3 2 1
- I feel that the tasks we do on this team are very exciting. 5 4 3 2 1
- I feel that the tasks we do on this team are personally meaningful. 5 4 3 2 1
- I believe our work makes a real difference in the lives of other people. 5 4 3 2 1
- Our team sets aside time every week to create ideas for the future. 5 4 3 2 1

Is my wider community, business, or organization a natural igniter of latent energy?

- Our executives ask questions that others find intriguing. 5 4 3 2 1
- Employees are given time to work on projects that excite them. 5 4 3 2 1
- I find the vision of this organization exciting and energizing. 5 4 3 2 1
- This organization encourages employees to come up with innovative ideas and suggestions. 5 4 3 2 1
- I believe that senior executives listen carefully to the ideas we have. 5 4 3 2 1
- It is the norm to arrange workshops and "away days" where the agenda encourages innovation. 5 4 3 2 1
- Employees are encouraged to read widely and to meet with different types of people. 5 4 3 2 1
- Internal networks include people who are really interesting. 5 4 3 2 1
- The tasks I work on resonate with my own values. 5 4 3 2 1

FIGURE 13.1 Igniting Latent Energy in the Three Areas of Your Work Life

The *Glow* Profile

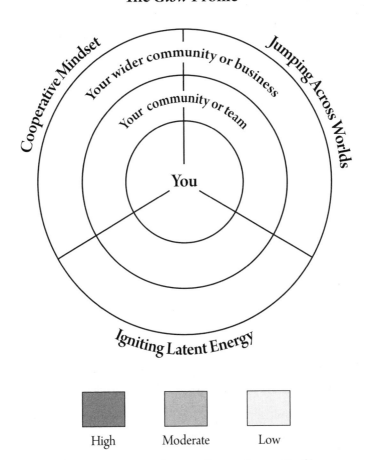

FIGURE 13.2 Your Igniting Latent Energy Profile

Once you have responded to all the statements in Figure 13.1, add up your ratings in each section; they will range from 9 to 45.

36 to 45 = high

26 to 35 = moderate

 9 to 27 = low

Now move to the *Glow* Profile in Figure 13.2. In the "igniting latent energy" segment of the figure, use different colors or a coding scheme such as the one shown to indicate the extent to which latent energy is ignited in the three areas of your work life.

Profile Type	Your Score	Team or Community Score	Wider Community Score
A	High	High	High
B	Moderate or High	Moderate	Moderate
C	Moderate or High	Low	Low
D	Low	Moderate or High	Moderate or High
E	Low	Low	Low

Interpreting the Igniting Latent Energy Profile

Take a look at your igniting latent energy profile, and select the type that is closest to yours:

Profile Type A: Your scores for igniting latent energy are high, and so are the scores for the team and the community

You are a natural igniter; you have a questioning way of looking at the world; you are curious and prepared to ask the big questions and to imagine how the world could be. So you are well positioned to ignite Hot Spots and have the ideas and excitement to draw people toward you and help them *Glow*.

Your igniting capabilities are reflected in your team or community, which has a naturally open and exciting way of looking at the world. You are on a team and in a community that are naturally igniters and are probably already buzzing with ideas and insights.

You may already be taking many of the recommended actions, but take a look at them to determine whether there is more you could be achieving.

Actions to Take You are in a great situation and have a wonderful opportunity to *Glow* and to find and flourish in Hot Spots. Review Actions 7, 8, and

9 (Chapters Fourteen, Fifteen, and Sixteen) to ensure there is not more you could be doing. Your main actions are to look at your analysis of cooperative mindset to ensure that you have sufficient cooperation to make the most of this tendency toward ignition, and at your analysis of jumping across worlds to be sure that you are involving a broad and creative group of people.

Profile Type B: Your score for igniting latent energy is moderate or high, and the team and community scores are moderate

If your score is moderate, your skill at igniting latent energy could be more developed, but you have the potential to be an igniter of energy, and taking action can develop this potential. If your score is high, you already have well-developed capabilities in this area. You are on a team or in a community that may not have the same strengths. Remember, though, that the team or community does have potential, and this potential can be developed.

Actions to Take   You have the great advantage of being a natural igniter of latent energy and now need to engage with others to encourage them to become more stimulating and sparky. Your first action is to engage them with these concepts—join with your colleagues as a learning group and discuss how to ask more igniting questions, create more compelling visions, and take a closer look at the tasks you are engaged in to find out if there is more you can do to create a meaningful and exciting environment.

Profile Type C: Your score for igniting latent energy is moderate or high, and the team and community scores are low

You are a natural igniter and have an instinctive way of asking questions and thinking about the future. You have the potential to find and flourish in Hot Spots. However, you have landed in a Country Club where the people around you are content to do the routine work rather than to *Glow*.

Actions to Take   You can support the team by sharing these diagnostics and engaging in a conversation about how to make your work more exciting. Action 9, crafting meaningful and exciting work, is a good place to start (see Chapter Sixteen). Then take a look at Actions 7 and 8 (Chapters Fourteen and Fifteen) to determine how you can start a conversation about asking the igniting questions and engaging with others in visualizing the future.

Profile Type D: Your score for igniting latent energy is low, and the team and community scores are moderate or high

Until now, you have not valued igniting latent energy and have been content to operate in a Country Club. But by remaining like this, you face the possibility of narrowing your options and reducing your capacity to be innovative and ultimately to *Glow*.

However, you now find yourself in a place where the people around you are prepared and willing to ask the igniting questions and create visions of the future. This represents a wonderful opportunity for you to engage with your colleagues to ensure that you leave the Country Club behind and start to *Glow*.

Actions to Take You are in a great position to build your igniting skills and habits because you have around you people who are engaged in igniting questions and visions. Take a look at Action 9 (Chapter Sixteen) to see what you can do about creating a more exciting job; then move to Action 7 (Chapter Fourteen) to take a closer look at the questions you could be asking of yourself and others. Finally, Action 8 (Chapter Fifteen) will help you think about opening your eyes to a longer-term vision.

Profile Type E: Your score for igniting latent energy is low, and so are the scores for the team and the community

You are in a classic Country Club, and you and your colleagues may even be enjoying the lack of excitement and energy. But my guess is that this is already frustrating you, and you are certainly not *Glowing*. So what are you going to do?

Action to Take Igniting latent energy is most effective as a team activity, so the best way to start would be to share this discussion with your teammates and also ask them to complete the diagnostics; their perspective may differ from yours. If you all agree that you are in a place that needs ignition, now is the time to start reenergizing. As a team, look first at the jobs you do and the tasks you engage in to identify what you might do to reenergize and ignite your work. Then move on to Actions 7 and 8 (Chapters Fourteen and Fifteen) to begin work on a broader agenda for change.

Key Points in Chapter Thirteen

The Third Principle: Igniting Latent Energy

You *Glow* by engaging with what's important and meaningful to you. Without this connection, your energy rapidly dissipates. This sort of spark of an idea was behind Ratan Tata's dream of a one-lakh car. Latent energy is ignited by asking questions that spark energy, by creating visions that compel, and by crafting meaningful and exciting work. A place where no one is igniting latent energy is a Country Club, where everyone seems to be happy but no one is *Glowing*.

In this chapter the *Glow* Profile helped you see where you stand with regard to your own attitudes and skills, your team's attitudes and competence, and the extent to which your company or community encourages you to ignite latent energy. From the profile you are able to determine which profile type is nearest to your own:

Profile Type A   You, the team you work with, and the wider community are very adept at igniting latent energy, which creates wonderful opportunities for you to *Glow*.

Profile Type B   You, your team, and the wider community are skilled in some aspects of igniting latent energy, so the emphasis is on increasing the level of ignition in our team.

Profile Type C   You are fairly adept at igniting latent energy, but you find yourself in a Country Club, where ignition is limited or nonexistent. Actions 7, 8, and 9 can all help awaken your colleagues from their torpor.

Profile Type D You are not a natural igniter of energy but find yourself surrounded by a relatively energized team or community, which presents a terrific opportunity for you to learn from others.

Profile Type E Neither you, your team, nor the larger community values igniting latent energy, which places you in a Country Club with low energy and little opportunity to *Glow*. Think about the effect this is having, particularly on innovation, and together work on Action 7, asking questions that spark energy, and Action 8, creating a visions that compel.

Chapter Fourteen

ACTION 7

Asking Questions That Spark Energy

People who Glow are adept at asking questions that spark energy, which requires courage and focus.

When you are able to engage with your own passion and beliefs, you become a source of energy for yourself and others. This energy is radiated to others as you *Glow* and ignites Hot Spots of innovation in your work community.

Look back at your igniting latent energy profile in Figure 13.1. It will help you understand where you are now with regard to asking the big, bold questions that generate energy. Also recall how Ratan Tata reached inside of himself and into his personal history and beliefs to find a question that was meaningful both to him and to everyone around him. His question "Why can't we create the one-lakh car?" was audacious, but it was not complex. In fact, it was a question that even a child could ask.

Think about how many times you have not asked a question because you thought it was too dumb or too simple. As Ratan Tata found, even the simplest of questions can have a profound impact. You can imagine that at the time some commentators probably thought that Tata—then in his early seventies—had lost his mind, that his proposal was simply the foolish ramblings of an older man. Yet because Tata was prepared to ask this question over and over and never deviate from it, people began to take him seriously.

In many ways this was a perfect igniting question because it was not too small, too obvious, or too inconsequential. This was a big, important, and meaningful question and had the potential to resonate with a diverse group of people. It's vital that igniting questions have multiple perspectives and can engage the interests of all sorts of people.

Igniting questions have always been marvelous creators of energy and innovation. There are times in the history of the world when whole communities have raised such questions. For example, the rise of romanticism in eighteenth-century Europe revitalized the then moribund Continent and paved the way for a dazzling burst of creativity in literature, the arts, the sciences, and philosophy. During this time, thinkers from Rousseau to Byron asked big, broad, igniting questions. What helped in this age of Enlightenment was that not only was it legitimate to ask big questions, but there was a whole infrastructure that had arisen to provide a forum for conversation. In salons and coffee houses in Vienna and Berlin, in Paris and Amsterdam, people talked, and many of the most profound contributions of that period arose from their conversations.

But how often in our lives of pragmatism do we simply focus on the day-to-day reality of living, eschewing broad "meaning of life" questions as irrelevant or a waste of time?

Reflect on how much your own focus on day-to-day work and solving immediate problems has resulted in your delegitimized deep, overarching questions. Do you feel that sometimes you have a preference for dealing with specifics and immediacies, perhaps in the belief that taking care of the parts will take care of the whole?

It seems to me that if you really want to *Glow*, the viselike grip of relentless pragmatism needs to be softened by the invigorating spirit of romanticism. Big, broad questions must be legitimized again as a driver of the constant endeavor not only to execute for today but also to renew for tomorrow.

As you reflected on Ratan Tata's story, you may have thought, "Well, that's fine for him. He is the head of an enormous company with extraordinary wealth, vast resources, and a history of philanthropy. What about me and my meager resources?" That's a legitimate reaction to the Tata story; he is indeed a man of immense resources. But you don't need immense resources to ignite latent energy by asking bold questions. In the story that follows, you will see how Johanna, with very few resources, went on to build an innovative and exciting job around having the courage to ask audacious questions.

The Story of a Creative Agency

I met Johanna early in her career before she went on to become the founder of a successful recruitment and selection business specializing in creative talent. Johanna was determined to succeed—she really wanted to be someone who radiated energy and *Glowed*. Using some of the techniques we will discuss later in this chapter, Johanna learnt to ask the big, audacious questions and from this draw out an inspiring vision. Here are some of the questions she asked at the very beginning that inspired her to *Glow*:

> *"Are people who work in the creative and artistic industries (such as Web designers and graphic artists) different from everyone else, and if so, in what ways?"*
>
> *"Should recruiting agencies treat people in the artistic and creative industries differently from everyone else?"*
>
> *"What do artistic and creative people want from a recruitment agency?"*
>
> *"In what new ways might the working lives of artistic and creative people be supported?"*

Johanna asked these questions of pretty much everyone she met and listened carefully to the conversations that ensued. She kept asking these questions even as she began to grow the business. Over time she developed a vision for the future of her business. Here is her initial vision:

Imagine a talent agency that really understood what it means to be a creative person, an agency that creative people see as their career partner, a resource that helps them understand themselves, brings them great opportunities, and supports them with a network of friends and colleagues. Imagine a talent agency that serves as a forum where creative people meet and that provides them with creative workspaces, contacts, and networks. Imagine an agency that creative people think of as their lifelong talent partner.

This is a great vision—it resonates with Johanna's personal beliefs, it is capable of generating meaning for her and her colleagues, and it has a sense of possibilities. These questions and the vision that Johanna created became the focal point for an energized Hot Spot in which Johanna and her staff *Glowed*. As the community grew, the vision and questions became the rallying point for igniting latent energy—just as Ratan Tata's vision had ignited the development of the Nano car. In Johanna's business, whatever her staff worked on, they always knew that their unique approach was to support and manage the careers of talented creative people.

Whether you realize it or not, you have big, igniting questions within your reach and inspiring visions in your head. The challenge is to form and access these questions and visions—and then to communicate them in a way that others find compelling and motivating.

To understand this point, let's take a closer look at what Johanna did. Like many of us, Johanna was not brought up to ask audacious questions. She grew up believing that the big questions were not her concern—either she didn't know enough or she should already know the answers or she should wait for someone else to ask them. From kindergarten onward, she was encouraged, as most children are, to rein in her natural talent to ask big questions. So to dare to ask the big, audacious questions as an adult, she had to jettison a lifetime of habits and replace them with new ones.

How much like Johanna are you? Are there times when you feel it is not your place to ask big questions? By steering away from big questions, you are significantly reducing the possibility of *Glowing* in Hot Spots.

So what are you going to do? Johanna was determined to create energy and excitement in her life. She knew instinctively that she would have to be inventive about the world. This is what Johanna did: She became a skilled hunter of information treasures. She created time and space for conversations. She cultivated her "third place"—a place beyond work and home. And she developed new rules. Together these four broad actions enabled her to ask the questions that became important to her personal development and the development of her business.

Hunting for Information Treasures

The questions Johanna asked were pretty tough, and to get to them, she had to broaden her thinking and conversations significantly. She did this in three ways. First, she made a habit every day to expose herself to an ever wider variety of information and stimuli. For example, she joined a pottery class and a yoga retreat so that she could generate independent and insightful thoughts about creativity. Next, she began to read more widely and made sure she did not limit herself to topics that were already familiar to her. By learning how others saw these issues, she was in a better position to widen her base of questions. For example, she began to read *Marketing Weekly* and one of the arts magazines. She also began to read the *Economist* to get a better understanding of current business issues. Finally, Johanna began to build stronger connections with experts in fields very different from her own. For example, she made the acquaintance of one of the professors at the Royal College of Art and made a point of going to its graduation celebrations, where she spent time talking with the graduates to get a sense of their career aspirations (and perhaps give them some pointers). She also made it a habit to keep in touch with people who knew more than she did. So she joined an entrepreneurship network and met a couple of established entrepreneurs, whom she asked to be her mentors.

If you want to ask the big, audacious questions, you must, as Johanna did, search for information treasures. What will help you come up with the sparking questions? Here are three actions you can take now to make sure you find those nuggets.

☼ Actions to take now to find information treasures

Action 7.1 *Opening up to new experiences.* Johanna widened her experiences by joining a couple of classes that she probably would not have done in the past and with people who are different from her and are likely to have the creative perspective that she is keen to develop. Take another look at the possible avenues in Action 5, jumping out of the boundaries that constrain you, and Action 6, finding and moving to boundaryless places, to see what you can do to broaden your experience (see Chapters Eleven and Twelve). Remember, though, that Johanna had some insight into the sorts of places and people who were most likely to yield information treasures; she knew that creative situations and creative people could be the stimulus for a sparky question. So as you think about broadening your experiences, keep in mind a sense of the broad themes that you believe your questions should be addressing.

Action 7.2 *Engaging in focused reading.* Books, blogs, and Web sites all are great hunting grounds for the information treasures that could really trigger a question. Again, think about the broad themes you are interested in (Johanna's were creative people and entrepreneurial acumen, among others), and research where you can learn more about them. Identify the two sources of information that you believe will broaden your knowledge most, and commit to reading these sources on a regular basis.

Action 7.3 *Connecting with experts.* Johanna took her creative values and ideas forward by deliberately finding occasions to meet with creative experts. That's why she started to hang out at the Royal College of Art and with the entrepreneurial network. She figured that both these communities would be great sources of information treasures. Glance back at Figure 10.2 in Chapter Ten and in particular look at Quadrant 3. As you review your communities, ask yourself whether any of them are allowing you to connect with people who are experts in the areas you are interested in developing. If not, identify two communities that have experts in them, and work out a plan for connecting with these communities.

The risk, of course, is that by broadening your thinking and asking more incisive questions, your constant questioning will lead to a highly politicized environment of second-guessing and point-scoring. The antidote to that risk is a relentless focus on what it is you and your colleagues are working on—in other words, a focus on purpose—to challenge each other vigorously but always in an appropriate way.

Creating Time and Space for Reflection

As I watched Johanna over the years, I could see that lack of time would be a real pitfall for her. She knew that she needed to broaden her knowledge, but at the same time, the minutiae of her day-to-day life often seemed to overwhelm her. Do you ever feel overwhelmed by the minutiae of your life? I know for myself that lack of time and appropriate space is one of the greatest barriers to deep conversations and times of reflection that could encourage me to ask the big questions.

Johanna recognized that this would be a problem and thought hard about her conversations. She realized that too many of them seemed to be brief exchanges in the corridor—dehydrated talk, as it was dubbed in Chapter Six. She acknowledged that constant interruptions and ringing phones gave her little time for real thought and conversation. She knew that if she wanted to have great conversations, she would need to be more alert and attentive, more relaxed and nonjudgmental, and fresher and able to think clearly. The way she was living her life was just not providing this for her. So she took two steps to create more time and space: she put time aside—her "golden hour"—and she thought hard about where and with whom she was spending her time.

She also realized that to have great conversations and to give herself time to reflect, she would have to change the locales in which she spent her time. Without an office in the early days, she was spending too much time on her own at home, working on her business ideas. So she joined a business club that attracted creative professionals, which served as a forum where she could meet like-minded people. Once a week, in the relaxed atmosphere of the club, she had the opportunity to strike up meaningful conversations with interesting people.

Take a look at the two actions that follow to decide whether these would help you clear away some of the dehydrated talk from your world and find a more engaging and stimulating forum for conversation.

Actions to take now to create space and time for reflection

Action 7.4 *Setting aside a "golden hour."* Looking back at some of the earlier actions in this book, you will see that taking time out of your business schedule is a recurring theme. In Action 2, mastering the art of great conversation, the emphasis was on putting time aside in your schedule to engage in conversation with others. In Action 5, jumping out of the boundaries that constrain you, there are a whole set of actions for allowing serendipity into your life: scheduling "golden moments," taking time out, and arranging minisabbaticals. Here my suggestion is the "golden hour," time you set aside every week specifically to devote to thinking and talking in pursuit of your big questions.

Action 7.5 *Finding new places.* The challenge here is to find a forum that is a place of relaxed conversation rather than another frenzied group. So take time to think about the themes you are interested in and then locate one forum that has a group of people who may also want to engage in serious conversation. In a sense, you need to find the modern equivalent of the eighteenth-century Viennese coffee house. Take time out every week, if possible, to spend with this group. And if one doesn't exist, consider forming one yourself. Circle back to the ideas regarding communities of practice in Action 5 (Chapter Eleven) to consider how you could best do this.

Cultivating Your "Third Place"

Johanna realized that no matter how much she tried to change her routines at work, it was always going to be hard to find space to reflect and think. If she was to create the vision and igniting questions capable of sparking a Hot Spot, she would have to make some radical changes. She began to think about a "third place," a place separate from work and home.

A "third place" has been crucial to my own ability to ask igniting questions. Think about your own life. So much of it is bounded by your roles and responsibilities at work and your duties at home. In my case, I know that being a professor at London Business School means I have to behave in particular ways, and at home, as a mother of teenage boys, I also have a whole host of obligations. The problem with these roles and responsibilities is that as enjoyable as they are, they leave me little time to reflect and mull over what I need to do in my own life apart from teaching and parenting. Everyone needs is a "third place" —a haven from work and home.

Johanna's "third place" was the yoga retreat she went on twice a year. Her daily half hour of yoga in the peace of her bedroom also provided a "third place" that gave her peace of mind and the space and time to think.

My own "third place" is my little Spanish apartment on the Mediterranean. It has its special history, its artifacts (simple furniture, just one iPod stocked with music I can write to), and a certain symbolism (a place of calm and isolation) that encourages me to think about the important issues that could lead to the big igniting questions. Each of us needs a "third place," unique and self-selected; without it, we lose our capacity to reflect and question. Note that the "third place" does not have to be a physical space, and even if it is, it can be a place shared with others where you experience moments of tranquility and calm in which you can catch your breath and reflect. Should you be doing more to create a "third place" that will allow you to discover those igniting questions that will encourage you to *Glow*? The actions that follow will help you discover if you need to do more to find and cultivate your "third place."

☼ Actions to take now to cultivate your "third place"

Action 7.6 *Selecting and developing your "third place."* Think about what could serve as your "third place." Here are some of the places people have told me about over the years:

> *"It's a cabin in the country where I can think and reflect."*
>
> *"It's the café I go to in the evening for an hour or two."*
>
> *"I find peace in the local tapas bar."*
>
> *"I think and reflect whenever I'm on an airplane."*
>
> *"My 'third place' is at the hairdresser's."*
>
> *"Once a week, I take a long walk in the country."*
>
> *"It's when I am jogging in the morning."*
>
> *"It's the peace I feel at the local church."*
>
> *"I take a one-week vacation twice a year."*
>
> *"I look forward to my walk along the beach every morning."*

Next, think about whether you want to extend or invest more in your "third place." Have you put sufficient energy and thought into your "third place"? If the answer is no, review the list of people's "third places" and see if they trigger some ideas of your own. Then decide whether you should focus on developing your existing "third place" or start from scratch and focus on a new one.

If you have a "third place" but have let it become overgrown or neglected, then now is the time to clear away the debris. If you have never allowed yourself the pleasure of a "third place," now is the time to give yourself permission to adopt one.

Developing New Rules

A "third place" can be a wonderful source of inspiration outside of work, but what about on the job? If your work life is frenetic and stressful, you may have to create within your work a space for these big igniting questions to emerge.

Making room for this space that will mean developing some new rules about the way you work.

Ask yourself, "What simple rules could break the frenetic pace of my work life?" Johanna asked herself this question and came up with two new rules: "Ditch the meetings" and "Drop the negative office gossip." She realized she was going to too many (often unproductive) meetings, so she decided to go only to meetings where she felt she could make a real difference.

Johanna also realized that getting too involved in negative office gossip was distracting her from really thinking. She realized that she worked with two people who were real "dampeners," and every time she spoke with them, she walked away feeling negative. So her second rule was to identify the small group of negative and energy-quenching colleagues and avoid them as much as possible.

Actions to take now to develop new rules

Action 7.7   Identifying your time wasters. Over the next month or two, make a quick note of the occasions when you feel you are in a situation where you are adding very little value. For Johanna, these were times when she seemed to be in endless meetings. Take a long, hard look at this list, and see which items on it you can ditch. In our discussion of Action 9, crafting meaningful and exciting work, in Chapter Sixteen, you will have another opportunity to think about how best to reframe your work. At the same time as you are making a note of your time-wasting activities, also make note of your time-wasting times with other people, times when you are engaged in dehydrated talk. Identify the people who are preventing you from having high-quality conversations and, as Johanna did, drop the negative office gossip.

So now you have become a skilled hunter of information treasures, you have created time and space for conversations, have cultivated a "third place," and have developed some new rules. Before you leave this action, let's flex your muscle with an exercise in asking igniting questions.

An Exercise in Asking Igniting Questions

Begin by making a list of what you believe to be the inspiring, meaningful themes and topics that really excite you right now.

To get your creative juices flowing, here are some big themes and questions that have in the past been the source of flourishing Hot Spots and wonderful opportunities to *Glow*:

- What does it mean to be a force for good?
- Are brands good or bad for the world?
- What can the Internet do for people all over the world?
- What does "work" mean, and what defines a great place to work?
- How can we make a one-lakh car?
- How can we build a $100 computer?
- What role can banks play in rural communities?
- What role can the major food companies of the world play in alleviating world poverty?
- How can we encourage all the people in the world to share their knowledge?

OK, these are big questions, perhaps far outside the scope of the themes and questions you are prepared to explore. But remember that each of these questions has sparked a Hot Spot and each was asked by somebody who *Glows*. So taking these themes as a cue, list the questions that are important to you right now. The scope or scale may be different from those I've listed, but the intensity will be just as sharp. Here are some questions that are on my own mind right now:

- What is going to be important to baby boomers like me over the next decade of our lives?
- Why is it so hard to work flexibly in companies and achieve a work-life balance?

- What would it take to create a community of people who are excited by Hot Spots?

- Why don't companies allow people to share jobs so that each can work a couple of days rather than a whole week?

Write your own list of questions right now. One way of checking them out is to ask colleagues and friends what they think of them. I like to get a group together and ask each member to prepare a question that is then presented to the group. The other group members give immediate feedback on how the question feels to them: waving their hands if it's a Hot Spot question, shrugging if it is boring, and shivering if it is a Big Freeze question. It's a great exercise with immediate feedback, and people quickly become better and better at asking igniting questions. So make sure that you hone your questioning skills by trying out ideas in your group—you may be surprised by the results!

Key Points in Chapter Fourteen

ACTION 7
Asking Questions That Spark Energy

Questions can be wonderful igniters of latent energy—particularly when they are big, important, consequential, and meaningful. Sadly, too often pragmatism means we focus on the day-to-day reality of living rather than the life-enhancing questions that permit us to *Glow*.

Becoming a Skilled Hunter of Information Treasures
This will help you broaden your awareness.

Action 7.1 Opening up to new experiences

Action 7.2 Engaging in focused reading

Action 7.3 Connecting with experts

Creating Time and Space for Conversation

This can help you avoid dehydrated talk and instead engage in the types of creative dialogue from which igniting questions can emerge.

Action 7.4 Setting aside a "golden hour"

Action 7.5 Finding new places

Cultivating Your "Third Place"

This is the place beyond home and work roles and responsibilities where you can reflect and think about the issues that are important to you and bring to the surface the questions that are in your mind.

Action 7.6 Selecting and developing your "third place"

Developing New Rules

These are the simple rules that could break the frenetic pace of your working life and give you more time to reflect on the big questions.

Action 7.7 Identifying your time wasters

Chapter Fifteen

ACTION 8

Creating Visions That Compel

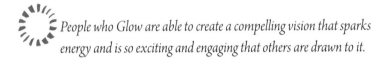 *People who Glow are able to create a compelling vision that sparks energy and is so exciting and engaging that others are drawn to it.*

A vision invites people into the future. It can describe what is important to you and can ignite the latent energy around you. Look back at your igniting latent energy profile in Figure 13.1 to help you to understand where you are now in terms of creating a compelling vision. Recall Ratan Tata's vision: "Imagine a world where rural communities can access the transport infrastructure so crucial for their development." It was a vision of the future so engaging and exhilarating that people were drawn to it in large numbers. Great visions like Tata's are palpable: they actually allow others to think their way into them.

Following are some of the ways I heard people talking about an igniting vision that helped them *Glow*:

> *"I could imagine so clearly where we were going—we knew what we had to do, and we were all excited about getting there."*

*"I had spent years dreaming about this. What really seemed to make a
     difference is that I was able to describe my dream so clearly that others
     could see what I was aiming at and wanted to become part of what I was
     building."*

*"I was really attracted to this because of the way the leader described her ideas
     about what we were creating. Her ideas were so vivid that I could clearly
     imagine what it would be like and the part I could play."*

The first person speaks of her own vision; the other two talk of being
inspired by a visionary leader. The secret to creating a Hot Spot in which
to *Glow* is to find a visionary person capable of igniting latent energy—and
that person might well be you, expressing your own visions and ideas about
the future.

You can find visionaries who ignite the latent energy around you. Think
of how Al Gore ignited thinking around the world on climate change. Or
how Nelson Mandela ignited thinking around equality and peaceful coex-
istence. These great charismatic sources of ignition are wonderful to experience, but because they are distant, they are unlikely to be sources of *Glow*
in your own life. To *Glow*, you need to tap into your own personal source of
igniting vision. In this chapter we examine what it will take for you to access
your courage, convictions, and values to bring your own nascent vision to the
fore and communicate it in a compelling way.

Mohi and a Vision That Compels

Mohi is a colleague whom I work with occasionally. He works for a large
company and sees his mission as helping the company innovate. Mohi is
a great source of visionary inspiration. Every time I meet him, I walk away
inspired, with exciting possibilities in mind. Recently, I have helped him
on a couple of projects because his vision made me eager to volunteer: the
Hot Spot he has created I find almost irresistible. Mohi *Glows* brightly. His
projects are always populated by fascinating people. In Mohi's projects I am

likely to meet film makers, musicians, professors of knowledge management, Japanese businessmen—there are no boundaries.

Whenever we are together, Mohi tells me about his visions. The table becomes covered with his ideas—diagrams of his plans, CDs of musicians he is working with, reports he is writing. Mohi is great at sharing his excitement and suggesting ways in which he thinks I might join in. How does Mohi do this? I see four characteristics that are crucial to the formulation of Mohi's vision:

- He is not afraid to ask the "what if" questions that get him thinking.

- He is prepared to spend time daydreaming.

- He is tightly connected to his own values and beliefs as sources of energy.

- He uses stories to weave dreams.

Asking the "What If" Questions

Visions are about the future—and a good way to begin to frame your thinking about the future is to go back to the ideas about questions but this time to phrase them as "what if" questions. Since "what if" questions are about events that have never taken place, you have to move beyond your conscious mind to access your ideas about possible futures. It is sometimes in your daydreams that you begin to rehearse possible futures and create a vision of what could ignite your energy. You ask and answer "what if" questions every time you dream.

"What if" questions are about the future, not the past. By changing the focus of your vision, they serve to weaken the links to the past and strengthen the links to the future. Thinking about the future is a much less analytical and rigorous task than thinking about the past. So rather than accessing your rational and analytical mind, as you do when you are asking questions and engaging in disciplined debate, you are engaging your imagination and accessing your dreams.

Working with Mohi, I see that these "what if" questions can be vital. For example, he has asked, "What if companies could join up to create an institute for cooperation?"

We can all ask "what if" questions. The challenge to overcome is that we have been trained to look only to the past and ask "what was" questions. So as adept as we may be at looking at what went before, at analyzing figures, spotting trends, figuring out what happened, future-oriented questions can be trickier.

☀ Actions to take now to ask "what if" questions

Action 8.1   *Asking "what if" questions.* Find a place where you can concentrate (your "third place"), and set aside a few hours (block these "golden moments" with your gold-ink pen) to let your imagination wander, writing down "what if" questions as they occur to you. When you are satisfied with your mental wandering, look at your questions, and decide if there are any that really ignite your imagination. Try those out on friends and see how others feel about them: do any ignite people's imagination?

Here are some questions that have settled into my mind over the past couple of years:

What if technology fundamentally changes the way we do business?

What if young people want something completely different?

What if cooperation, rather than competition, became the normal way of working?

What if we were able to create virtual ways of working?

My guess is that as you look at these questions some will ignite you while others will leave you cold. You have to build your own list—here are some more questions friends have come up with:

What if supermarkets donated all unsold foodstuffs to homeless shelters and soup kitchens one day before the expiration date in exchange for a tax credit?

What if Election Day were made a national holiday so that everyone could vote without missing work?

What if all elected posts in local government were required to be nonpartisan?

What if consumers were fined for not recycling?

Giving Time to Daydreaming

Great ideas and visions are part unconscious insight, part external inspiration. It is the back-and-forth between insight and inspiration that serves as a basis for refining your ideas and using stories to weave dreams. Sometimes the greatest source of insight will come from something you have heard, an idea you have seen, or an emotion you have felt. The information treasures we thought about in Action 7 (Chapter Fourteen) can be important fuel for your vision. Sometimes the greatest treasure comes in small bits of information that are unusual and worthy of attention. It is these bits of unusual information that taken together can build on your unconscious ideas or provide other avenues for action. For example, when I was in Mumbai in 2008, I made it my habit to read the daily newspapers. What caught my notice was an item about the Nano car. It was this information treasure that led me to the whole Nano story. Catching these small nuggets of unusual and worthy information can be important steps in helping you elaborate your dreams.

Learning to daydream was an important way that Mohi learnt to *Glow*. He kept his energy alight by spinning the dreams that became his vision for how his work could develop. He did this by connecting with his memories—not of the past but his "memories of the future." These are the stories he could tell himself about what the future could be and how he could create a place of high energy and innovation.

Mohi wanted to access more of his creative side. He knew that creating a vision of how the company could innovate would need his personal creativity. He had heard that poets often sleep with a pencil and paper by the bed to make notes as soon as they wake up. He resolved to do the same, and every now and again, he was surprised in the morning by a creative insight he had had during the night.

Thinking about how I daydream, I realized long ago that I am a morning person. By the afternoon, my mind is usually so distracted by the minutiae of my life that my chances of being reflective are very low. So I tend to put aside a couple of morning hours every week. These are my "golden moments," blocked out in my calendar in gold ink. When I glance at my schedule, I can see the golden notations, and somehow the majesty of the color decreases my temptation to fill that reflection time with the spillover of everyday life.

☼ Actions to take now to help you daydream

Action 8.2   *Daydreaming.* Acknowledge that daydreaming can help you imagine and describe the future. You can elaborate your "memory of the future" by making it as tangible as possible. Ask yourself these three questions:

- What would people see?
- How would they feel about it?
- What would it mean to me?

Next, think about the periods in your life when you have felt particularly creative and able to access your innermost thoughts. Could you re-create these periods on a more frequent basis? Would the pencil-and-paper-by-the-bed habit work for you?

Connecting to Your Values and Beliefs

When you *Glow*, you capture the imagination of others with your ideas, your visions, or your stories. People are drawn to those that resonate with themselves. They want to hear the "real you" rather than a made-up, fabricated you.

Authenticity is natural; you don't have to work at it. But what you do have to do is have sufficient self-knowledge that you don't stray into attitudes or behaviors that are not the authentic you. If your vision does not reflect your own values and beliefs, you will jettison it at the first sign of difficulty. And if your vision does not reflect your values, others will also abandon it at the first sign of trouble. To create resonant questions and visions, you have to connect them with your values and beliefs, and this means that you need to make that connection clear and actively build your self-awareness.

☀ *Actions to take now to connect to your values and beliefs*

Action 8.3   *Connecting to your heart.* To connect more fully to your values and beliefs, you need to hear what your heart has to say—and also what your friends have to say:

- First, ask yourself what words your closest friends and associates would use to describe your values.

- Then ask, "When I reflect on the decisions I have made in the past, what underlying values and beliefs have steered these decisions?"

- Use both questions to draw up a list of the values and beliefs that are important in your life.

- When you begin to daydream around a vision or to ask an igniting question, go back to these values and beliefs and ask yourself, "Does what I am thinking about embody what it important and valuable to me?"

Take a look at Action 9.4 in Chapter Sixteen for a list of values that people often hold about their work.

When Mohi reflected on these questions, he realized that one of his core values was the creativity of synthesis. He knew that any vision he created would have to resonate with his own creative spirit. When I ask myself these questions, I know that to remain authentic to myself, I need to create questions and visions that reflect with my own values and beliefs around building communities, focusing on innovation, being autonomous, and creating a balanced life. So when I built a vision about how the ideas around Hot Spots would evolve, the vision was of a community of people engaged in state-of-the-art work, many of whom worked part-time and lived in the place they most loved. That meant, of course, that there were other visions I rejected as being inauthentic to my beliefs and values. So, for example, my vision was not of building a consulting practice, because a balanced life is an important value to me, and I knew that managing many people would destroy this and the autonomy I prize. Connecting to your values and beliefs is about making choices—and sometimes the most crucial choices are about what to reject.

Using Stories to Weave Dreams

People like Mohi and Johanna, who have created a future vision that others find compelling, often use stories to ignite and inspire others. These stories can take many forms—they could be about how the idea will be developed, how it will look when it is completed, or what it will feel like to others as they become involved. The more engaging, inspiring, and interesting the story, the more likely others will be drawn to it and prepared to engage their energy. When you build a story about the future, you allow and encourage others to engage in your narrative. People begin to see themselves in your story of the future and weave their own dreams as you weave yours.

Weaving stories was one of the ways that both Mohi and Johanna connected with others. For Johanna, this meant creating her vision of the future by taking an idea that was important to her and part of her personal store of dreams and visions. The dream she had was of an informal work setting where people could flow in and out. She thought of the open-air markets she had seen in California where people brought their produce to trade and sell. She used this initial idea to spin a story by imagining how this market would work if instead of food and wine, people brought their skills and crafts. So she imagined a Web designer laying out a stall with some of his designs. Prospective clients would wander around "sampling" the product before they engaged the Web designer.

When Johanna described this dream and story to others, they could understand it. They to could picture the market scene and the stalls. They could imagine themselves in the market for skills, and they could imagine how they felt and what contribution they could make.

Mohi also found a way of describing his vision through a story. The story and image he told was of the Japanese tea ceremony. For him, this ceremony captures many of his impressions of innovation. To tell the story to others, he collaborated with one of Japan's most revered film makers to produce a short film about the tea ceremony. I was in the audience when the film was first shown and found it immeasurably moving. It begins with the tea master delicately trimming the leaves of the trees around the ceremonial place to achieve the perfect dappling effect of light and dark. Then the teapots are taken out and carefully arranged, the water is boiled on a simple fire, and the tea for the occasion is selected. From a story lasting less than five minutes, the audience began to understand what Mohi and his colleagues believed in.

This story of the tea ceremony resonated with the values of quality, simplicity, and tradition. The story resonates with Mohi because it encapsulates the values that drive him—the values of innovation through simplicity and acknowledging the traditions of the past. By developing this story, Mohi had created a way of talking with others about what they could do to create innovation and ultimately to *Glow*.

Actions to take now to create a resonating story

Action 8.4   *Creating resonating stories.* In your questions and visions, you have begun to think about a theme for the future that could be important and resonant with you. Now imagine that theme as a story. It could be a realistic story about how your vision will develop, in the way that Johanna used the story about the California market to describe her ideas, or it could be an analogy that alludes to an aspect of your vision, in the way that Mohi used the tea ceremony as an analogy of the simplicity he thought would be crucial to innovation.

Now write the outline of the story or analogy that illustrates what you are excited about—no more than one page. Test the story out with friends, Does it resonate with them? Does it capture what is important? Would they want to be part of it?

An Exercise in Crafting an Igniting Vision

The challenge here is to think about your vision for the future and begin to tell it as a compelling and resonant story. How will the events emerge? Who will be involved? What will they experience, and what will be their perceptions and emotions? How will you and others feel? These stories will come from your dreams and have resonance through their connections to your deeply held values and beliefs.

So let's make a story out of one of the visions you have accessed. I've always enjoyed children's stories in which you can insert your own names for the characters. I have used this same idea to write a little story into which you can drop your own characters, your own product, and your own vision. Play around with it, and use it as a basis for creating a more authentic and vibrant story of your own.

Once upon a time there was a (product/service/idea) that became really important to people and created an experience that they had never had before. This (product/service/idea) had been developed by a bunch of people who just knew that they were right (people like X, Y, and Z, who really cared about this and valued it). For months they toiled at the development, bringing in ideas and insights from around the world. Finally, it was ready to launch. They threw a party and invited everyone who had been involved in the design and also the clients they thought might find it useful. The party was a great success. Clients loved what the team had done; they realized this would give them something they had never had before. That evening as the sun went down, the team members got together to congratulate themselves on the success of the launch and to prepare for the hard work ahead.

That probably sounds more like a fairy tale than a realistic story. But it captures the elements of a story about the future. Reading the story, how did you feel? I wrote a story a little like this for my own team when I was launching the Hot Spots Movement because for me it is positive, it tells people something about the emotions they feel, and it conveys the values involved in the creation of the product, service, or idea. And as I write this piece, we have just had our first magical summer party where we sat with well-wishers beneath a beautiful canopy of branches and enjoyed the night air.

Key Points in Chapter Fifteen

ACTION 8
Creating Visions That Compel

When you create a vision, you are creating an invitation to the future. This can have a profound impact on drawing others to you and can ignite latent energy and help everyone *Glow*. People who create visions are not afraid to ask "what if" questions.

Asking "What If" Questions
Invite people into the future.

Action 8.1   Asking "what if" questions

Giving Time to Daydreaming
This can be an important source of compelling visions.

Action 8.2   Daydreaming

Connecting to Your Values and Beliefs
People are drawn to your ideas and vision for the future because they can see in these your true authentic self.

Action 8.3   Connecting to your heart

Using Stories to Weave Dreams

The more engaging and inspiring a story, the more people can see themselves in the story and feel compelled by it.

Action 8.4   Creating resonating stories

Chapter Sixteen

ACTION 9

Crafting Meaningful and Exciting Work

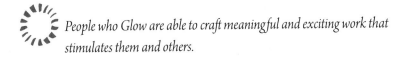 *People who Glow are able to craft meaningful and exciting work that stimulates them and others.*

Visions and questions are excellent aids to keeping you ahead of the curve and helping you *Glow*. Mohi's vision of the innovative company, Ratan Tata's vision of the one-lakh car, and Johanna's vision of the creative job agency were all wonderful stimulators of energy—but to sustain energy over the longer term, you also need to be able to design your work and the jobs and projects you do in a way that brings meaning and excitement to you.

Think back to the experience of Harry and Julie in the creation of the chocolate-smelling deodorant spray, recounted in Chapter Nine. The vision was compelling, the questions were exciting, and their initial friendship and conversations sparked the igniting ideas—but to sustain their interest over the longer term, the work they engaged in had to be meaningful and exciting. For Harry and Julie, the work they embarked on really stretched their competence: after all, to encapsulate a chocolate aroma in deodorant form is fiendishly difficult. Our noses are very attuned to what chocolate smells like, so any sense of the artificial will turn people off. Thus the team faced a task that was novel, had few precedents, and would bring challenges that had never been faced before.

Visions and questions are great initial sparks to ensuring that you *Glow*, but to remain energized and innovative over a long period of time requires a day-to-day spark. That's why sparking tasks of the sort that Ratan Tata created are so important.

When the vision is a distant memory and the question begins to fade, tasks are what we do when we come to work in the morning, and they are what we are engaged in when we stay late into the evening; it is the tasks that help us *Glow*.

Tasks are the parcels of time, activities, and outcomes that define your working life. One of the reasons you *Glow* is because you are engaged in something that resonates with you. These tasks can be as straightforward as my working with Oriol to design the Hot Spot Chocolates or as complex as creating the one-lakh car. You *Glow* when you are engaged with tasks that are sufficiently complex that they capture your imagination or sufficiently meaningful that they capture your heart.

Complex Work That Captures Your Imagination

I sometimes wonder whether we underestimate the power of human endeavor and curiosity. How many times have you worked on a task that has been so sanitized, homogenized, and simplified that what you are left with is mind-bogglingly boring? You have been told in detail what to do, a job description has been drawn up and discussed with you, you have been told how to do the work, and you have been given performance evaluations to clarify what the expected outcomes are. At the end, you feel wrung out: where, you cry, is the initiative, the creativity?

You will never be ignited by these homogenized, sanitized tasks. Why? Because you—anyone—can do these tasks with your eyes shut—you can do them in your sleep. These tasks have been chopped up into such small pieces they can never become the sparks that ignite latent energy. You wish you were *Glowing*, but you feel like an automaton.

The latent energy that you and others have is much more likely to be sparked if the task you are engaged in is complex, ambiguous, and difficult. The ambiguity resides in the fact that it is not clear at first glance how the task can be performed successfully—you have to work with others to solve the puzzle, and perhaps even persuade volunteers to come and solve the puzzle with you. Thus an ambiguous task demands collaboration and teamwork. Think back to how intensely rewarding this can be and how much potential these moments have to ignite a Hot Spot and make you *Glow*. I heard this over and over again when talking to people who *Glowed*:

> *"The excitement was that this is a really tough nut to crack—it had lots of different parts, and we had no idea how to solve this problem when we began."*

> *"The job we were doing had never been done before—it was really engaging since we all had to work together to make it happen."*

> *"What I love about this is that everyone said it could not be done; the timelines looked as if they were impossible, and we knew all the time that we were up against the clock—this was new territory, and that caused a real buzz."*

Meaningful Work That Captures Your Heart

When your questions and visions resonate with your values and beliefs, you *Glow*, and it shows in your work. When you and others are engaged in a task that resonates with your values and beliefs, you are more likely to *Glow*.

The one-lakh car Hot Spot remained alight for four years because the task was complex and engaging—but also because this was a task that had meaning for the many hundreds of people who worked on it. Imagine how it felt to be working on a car that you knew your relatives in your home village could use.

Tasks don't have to be immense or profound for you to find meaning in them. Take my Hot Spot Chocolates story, for example. Designing chocolates for books could hardly be described as meaningful in the greater scheme of things. However, the task created an opportunity for me to *Glow* because it was meaningful to me personally. Creating Hot Spot Chocolates resonated with my own values and my sense of myself. I guess I see myself as a little creative, somewhat quirky, and a bit eccentric. So the idea of chocolates designed for a book was sufficiently quirky to resonate with my own self-image and values. I hear this same resonance when people talk about tasks in which they have *Glowed*.

> *"It was one of the most important moments of my working life. We all felt totally committed to what we where doing."*

> *"I really care about this—it is part of my beliefs and values—so the opportunity to work on this was profoundly exciting to me."*

> *"Since I was a kid, I wanted to do this—and when a bunch of people came along with me, it was just fabulous."*

What really strikes me in these comments is that people are personally engaged with something that resonates with them, something that has meaning to them and reflects their personal values.

Meaningful tasks that can ignite latent energy can spring from your self-image, values, and passions—so the meaning comes from inside. Meaning can also emerge from outside of you, through what is meaningful in your context, on the team, or in the company or the community. Tasks are meaningful to you because you can see that through their accomplishment you can make a difference—they have a consequence beyond you.

Not all tasks are meaningful and consequential—and of course, they don't need to be. In our heart of hearts, we know that many of the tasks we are involved in are important in a rather routine, mundane way but really have very little impact or consequence over the longer term. That's fine—but remember that these tasks are not the ones that will ignite latent energy, and you will not *Glow* as you accomplish them. So you need to balance them with tasks that are more meaningful for you.

One impediment to creating interesting and meaningful work is the conviction that you are so busy, you don't have time for anything else. If that is so, before you can think about making your work more exciting and meaningful, you may have to clear away some of the debris and face the problem of overdemanding work.

Facing the Problem of Overdemanding Work

Figure 16.1 presents a model for thinking about work that you may find useful as you consider how best to clear away the debris that stops you from working on complex and meaningful tasks. Since most of your work probably involves other people, my suggestion is that you share these ideas with your colleagues and go through the exercises and action points together.

In the figure you can see your work as a core with an outer boundary around it. At the core of the job or the task are the demands and obligations that everyone who does the job or task is obliged to meet. For example, in my job as a professor at London Business School, I am obliged to teach for a certain number of days each year and write a certain number of research articles. It was part of the deal when I took the job. In the actions that follow,

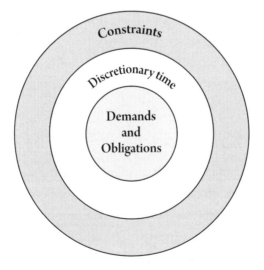

FIGURE 16.1. A Model of Your Work

you will have an opportunity to review the demands and obligations of your work and make efforts to understand them and possibly reduce them.

At the very outer limits of the job is a boundary that defines the limits of how you currently do your work. This outer limit could be defined by your current competencies, the resources you have currently available to you, or the time you have. These are the constraints. Last year I realized that one of the constraints I face as a typical baby boomer is that I don't have technology coursing through my veins in the way my teenage sons do. This was constraining my attempts to extend my work and make it more exciting by building a participative Web-based community around my ideas. So I am currently reducing this constraint by learning to use community-based technology and working with technological people.

Between the innermost core of demands and the outermost boundary of constraints is a space we might call your discretionary time. This is your room for maneuvering, the space you can play in, where you can craft the job any way that you want. You can make it more interesting, more meaningful, more complex, and even more fun. For example, in my own discretionary time, I have spent a significant amount of my time building a virtual movement around the idea of Hot Spots. My contract at London Business School does not oblige me to do this, and I have some (although not all) of the resources to make it happen. It's in that space I have a lot of fun and excitement and often feel that I am *Glowing*.

The trick to creating exciting, meaningful work is to increase your discretionary time as much as possible so that you have space for the exciting and the meaningful.

Mapping Demands and Constraints

When Johanna first worked with her colleagues to build the creative agency, she realized that the demands and constraints of the job gave her little discretionary time to take some of the actions that would make her task more exciting and innovative.

She had attracted a small team—Rajan, José, and Brian—to work with her, and each was as passionate as she was about the creative industry. As they began working together and tackling day-to-day tasks, they implicitly developed a sense of the demands of the job, primarily the following:

- It's important we dress in a creative way (being "on brand" is crucial).

- We must allocate time outside the office to meet with and network with creative people. So we should go to gallery openings and art shows to make sure we understand the creative industry.

- When we work with creative clients, our interactions with them must be clear and thoroughly followed up. We don't want the reputation of being a disorganized bunch of semicreative people.

- We must each interview at least twenty candidates a day if we are to become financially viable.

- We must write up in-depth interview notes and file them on a daily basis.

- We must be in the office by 9 A.M. at the latest.

- We must work from the office at all times.

These all seem to them to be realistic demands. However, as time went on, it became clear to Johanna that the team was beginning to lose energy and *Glowing* less brightly. The vision was still compelling and the questions were still intriguing, but the people around her were increasingly overburdened with the demands of the work and had little discretionary time to bring their own ideas and inspiration. When Johanna and her team examined the constraints, they found three that severely reduced their opportunity for discretionary time:

- We are constrained by financial resources and must all interview at least twenty candidates a day if we are to become financially viable.

- We are constrained by our competence: we would like to systematize some of the data collection but don't have the skills to do so.

- We are constrained by having to be in the office from 9 to 5.

Making Space for Meaning and Excitement

As the team members looked at the demands and constraints of their work, they asked themselves two questions: Are we overspecifying the job demands? And are we overestimating the constraints of the job?

By answering both questions, Johanna and her team were able to redesign their work to provide sufficient discretionary time for reflection and innovation, which in turn made their everyday tasks more meaningful and interesting to them. Let's look at what they did to make more space for meaning and excitement.

First, they looked at each of the demands of the job and asked themselves whether they really had to meet that demand. This revealed that many of the demands were responses to a major financial constraint, the cost of renting the office. They had taken a short lease on an office in central London, and paying the rent had become a major burden. So they decided to look around town for alternatives and found a shared office space at a fraction of their central London rent. By moving to this shared office, they were able to reduce their financial burden and gained the additional advantage of working with a network of creative people.

Next, they began to question the demand for them to be in the office between the hours of 9 and 5. They realized that many of their potential clients would actually prefer to meet in the evening rather than during the day. So they decided to draw up a team schedule showing when each team member was available for interviews. They also agreed to two mornings of "core time" each week when they would all be present at the office and hence available for meetings and discussion as a team.

Finally, they saw that some of the more mechanistic demands of their job were driven by technological constraints: lack of computer skills. So they agreed that the next person they would bring onto the team would have a background in information technology. Once their new IT colleague was on board, they were able to build a more efficient way of storing interview data and so free up more of their time for actual recruiting and interviewing work.

By reducing the demands and constraints of their work and increasing their discretionary time, each team member was able to conduct more interesting and more meaningful work, opening the opportunity to *Glow*. José was able to bring his fascination with the fashion industry into his work by spending time with fashion experts and at design school fashion shows. The close relationship he has built with the fashion community has been great fun for him and paid off for the company, which has become the first port of call when fashion students are job-hunting. Brian was able to bring his excitement about the potential of technology to fruition by building a Web presence that boosted interest in the creative agency.

Actions to take now to create space in your working life

Action 9.1 *Mapping demands.* Set aside time with your immediate colleagues to make a list of the current demands of the job you do. Take a look at Johanna's list of demands as a staring point. Remember that demands are the ways of working and the tasks that you believe anyone doing your job would be required to do. Then taking each demand in turn, ask the following questions:

- Is this demand crucial to the performance of the job?
- Have we overspecified this demand?
- What would it take to reduce this demand?

Action 9.2 *Mapping constraints.* Next, list what you believe are the key constraints of the work—time, money, equipment, skills, and so on. Again, taking each constraint in turn, ask the following questions:

- What impact is this constraint having on my working life?
- Is this a realistic constraint, and what could we do to reduce it?

Creating space at work is best done with strong, trusting relationships within your group and a network of acquaintances outside the group. Creating space is about pushing boundaries, shrinking unhelpful demands, and transforming tasks and relationships into sources of ignition.

Creating Meaningful and Exciting Work

Now that you and your colleagues have increased your discretionary time, you have space to craft more meaningful and exciting work. Remember that tasks that ignite latent energy have at least one of the following characteristics:

- The work is sufficiently complex to capture your imagination (like the chocolate-smelling deodorant).

- The work has personal meaning and resonates with your values (like the underlying creativity theme in Johanna's recruitment agency).

- The task has impact—you believe that it will make a difference to you or the company (like Ratan Tata's one-lakh car).

So as you go about making work more conducive to igniting latent energy, keep each of these in mind. Let's first take a look at these three possible characteristics of igniting tasks.

Crafting Complex Work That Captures Your Imagination

You *Glow* when you are engaged in complex work that captures your imagination. Complex work stretches your thinking, pushes the boundaries of your skill, and encourages you to broaden your networks to find solutions. However, there is a limit to whether complex tasks can motivate and sustain you as you *Glow*. When tasks become too complex for you and your colleagues to perform in a successful and satisfactory way, they become overwhelming and frustrating rather than engaging and exciting. Figure 16.2 provides a simple way to think about the relationship between complexity and frustration. You will *Glow* when you find that optimal point of complexity at

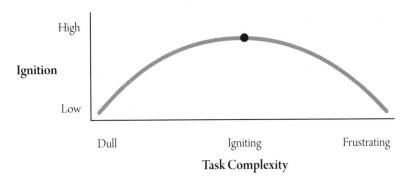

FIGURE 16.2 Task Complexity and Ignition

which a task becomes a real force for igniting latent energy and possibly fueling a Hot Spot. Below that optimal point, and the task is too simple to engage and excite you; above that optimal point, and it becomes too complex, more a point of frustration than a point of ignition. You should be focusing on achieving the optimal point.

Actions to take now to identify the optimal point of complexity

Action 9.3   *Mapping complexity.* Think about your work and the tasks you perform. Plot each of these tasks on the complexity graph in Figure 16.2.

- For tasks that are very simple and probably dull, ask yourself whether this is a task that needs to be done. If it does, try to make it as routine as possible.

- For tasks that you are finding too complex, think about ways to remove some aspects of the complexity. Are there other people in your extended network whom you might ask for help? Or is it possible to chunk your work into more manageable parts so that it is not so overwhelmingly complex?

- For tasks that are at optimal complexity, consider whether you can enlarge these tasks and make them more central to your daily life.

Crafting Meaningful Work That Resonates
with Your Values

Now you have created more scope in your work, how are you going to make
it more meaningful? Your work is meaningful when it resonates with and
reflects your personal values. As I have shown, as you learn to *Glow*, you will
consider the role that your values play in your work—as a source of thinking about cooperation and as a way of framing the relationships that will
be crucial to you. Here your values act as the core around which you can
construct meaningful work. We each have our own unique values, and so
what is meaningful for you may not be meaningful to another person. Your
challenge is to understand what is valuable for you and to ensure that at least
some of those values come through in your work.

☼ *Actions to take now to create more*
meaningful work

Action 9.4   *Identifying your work values.* First, make a note of the values that
are central to your work. You may want to look back to Action 8.3 in Chapter
Fifteen, in which you thought about how your friends would describe your
values. Following is a list of work values that people often find important;
pick the two that have the greatest resonance with you:

- The opportunity to make a real difference to those around me

- To work on something that I believe does good for the world

- Being able to work to a high degree of excellence

- Having a great deal of autonomy to work on what interests me

- Being creative at work

- The opportunity to support others through coaching and
  mentoring

- The opportunity to create something that I am proud of

- Having friends I can trust

- Stability and lack of stress

- The opportunity to provide for myself and my family

Action 9.5   *Placing your values at the core of meaningful work.* Focus on the two values that resonate most deeply with you, and ask yourself these three questions:

- Do these values play a role in my current work?

- What aspects of my work are nearest to them?

- What could I do now to extend those aspects of my work to more fully encompass these values?

Recall how in the creative agency José redefined his work so that he could spend more time at fashion shows. In doing so, José crafted work that was more meaningful to him and that resonated more fully with his work values of creativity.

Crafting Impactful Work That Makes a Difference

You *Glow* when you believe that the work you do has a positive impact on yourself or others. Think back to the Tata workers and their knowledge that the cars they made would help India's rural community immensely. Impactful work comes from a vision that engages and excites you and work that resonates with your own values. Impactful work also comes when you understand the effect your work has on others. (Would the workers in the Tata automobile factory have been so motivated and energized if they had no idea what they were building?) To make your work more impactful, you need to build stronger and more feedback-rich relationships with the broad network of people who are influenced by your work. This feedback helps you understand the impact of your work. The feedback may not all be positive, but the positive feedback provides a wonderful opportunity for you to *Glow*.

Johanna worked hard to make the work of her team more impactful. One of the ways she did this was by linking the experiences of her clients to the day-to-day experiences of her team. She asked successfully placed candidates to give the team feedback about their experience of the recruitment process. She then made sure that the feedback was shared by everyone. She also asked clients to tell stories about their new jobs. Johanna and the team then posted some of these stories on a bulletin board to remind everyone in the office of the impact their work had on the lives of their clients. So even on the bleakest or most hectic days, team members can read the stories on the wall and be reminded that they are making an important difference in people's lives.

Actions to take now to create more impactful work

Action 9.6 *Understanding and getting closer to your stakeholders.* To understand the impact of your work requires that you understand whose lives you are affecting. Think about these three areas of impact, and jot down some notes about the people involved:

- People who supply a service to you and your team
- Your customers and clients
- The wider community that could be affected by your work

Now think about who your stakeholders are and what you can do to make your work with them more meaningful and consequential. Here are three actions you can take:

- Ask them what impact your work has had on them.
- Discuss your hopes and aspirations for your work with them.
- Think of ways to link your work more closely with their needs.

By reaching out into your community, you are better able to create work that is impactful and creates an atmosphere in which you can *Glow*.

Key Points in Chapter Sixteen

ACTION 9

Crafting Meaningful and Exciting Work

Visions and questions are great energy-igniting sparks that help you *Glow*, but to remain energized and innovative and keep the flame alive, you need meaningful and exciting work. Tasks are the activities and outcomes that define your working life. One of the reasons you *Glow* is because you are engaged in doing something that really resonates with you.

Facing the Problem of Overdemanding Work

Often work lacks meaning and excitement because you are overwhelmed by the minutiae of day-to-day demands. So the first stage is to clear some of the debris from your current work and face the problem of overdemanding work.

Action 9.1　　Mapping demands

Action 9.2　　Mapping constraints

Crafting Complex Work That Resonates Your Imagination

The latent energy that you and others have is much more likely to be sparked if the task you are engaged in at work is complex, ambiguous, and challenging.

Action 9.3　　Mapping complexity

Crafting Meaningful Work That Resonates with Your Values

Such work reflects your values and resonates with you.

Action 9.4　　Identifying your work values

Action 9.5　　Placing your values at the core of meaningful work

Crafting Impactful Work That Makes a Difference

You can see that this work is making a difference in people's lives and thus has positive consequences beyond yourself.

Action 9.6　　Understanding and getting closer to your stakeholders

Chapter Seventeen

Glowing Every Week

I hope by now you are *Glowing* more. You've completed your *Glow* Profiles and understood what might be working for and against you. You've identified which of the nine actions are going to make a difference and have begun to acquire the habits and competencies of your key actions. Keeping on the path is about focusing your energy.

Staying on the Path

Much of what you have thought about in this book is designed to increase the stock of positive energy available to you at any point in time. The challenge you face is to ensure that all the actions you take focus rather than dissipate your energy. In the course of this book you have met a host of people who have been able to create and flourish in Hot Spots in their working life. For all of them, the capacity to focus their energy was crucial to their success. Having watched people who *Glow* over long periods of time, I see that they stay on the path by focusing on the journey forward, by removing the obstacles on the path, and by keeping track of progress.

Keep Defining What Is Important to You

Our lives have their own rhythms, and there will be times when more energy is available than at other times. I know for myself that when my kids were young, a great deal of my energy went into caring for them, and I was content to look for other people's Hot Spots and flourish in them. Now that my children need me less, I have more energy available to create my own Hot Spots. What I have seen in myself and others is that focusing on what is important is essential to staying on the path.

Be Vigilant for Distractions and Obstacles

On your journey, distractions and obstacles will litter your path. Don't let them slow your progress; push on through, actively removing the impediments in your way. A wonderful way of conceptualizing this is to think of the journey of Odysseus, hero of Homer's *Odyssey*.

In Homer's story, Odysseus has been journeying for many years and is now set on returning home. His path takes his boat and crew across dangerous straits. The journey is perilous, and few sailors ever come through alive because they are distracted by the seductive songs of the Sirens, who entice the seamen into their watery graves. Here is Circe, the sorcerer-goddess, telling Odysseus what to expect:

> First you come to the Sirens, who bewitch everyone who nears them. If any man draws near in his innocence and listens to their voices, he never sees home again; never again will wife and children run to greet him with joy for the Sirens bewitch him with their melodious song.

Odysseus is determined to journey through the straits alive and also to experience the wondrous sound of the Sirens. Circe warns him:

> Go past that place, and do not let the men hear: you must knead a good lump of wax and plug their ears with the pellets. If you wish to hear them yourself, make the men tie up your hands and feet and fasten your body tight to the mast, and then you can enjoy the song as much as you like. Tell them that if you shout out and command them to let you loose, they must tie you tighter with a few more ropes.

Thanks to Circe's advice, Odysseus and his crew were able to sail through the straits and return home. The wax in the ears of the sailors and the rope around Odysseus's hands and feet were sufficient to avoid the distractions of the Sirens.

There will be distractions on your journey, although they are unlikely to come in such an attractive form as the Sirens. People will say that cooperation is "unfocused" or that it's not up to you to ask the big questions or that you should focus on the immediate team. Like Odysseus, you will have to consciously and intentionally reduce these distractions—perhaps by avoiding these people, perhaps by spending time with the energizers around you rather than the distractors.

Use the *Glow* Checklists

One way of staying on the path to ensure that you *Glow* is to check your status and your progress periodically. The checklist presented here consists of thirty questions that will help you plot your path. The checklist contains three sets of ten questions, corresponding to the three circles of the *Glow* Profile:

The first asks, "Are you doing enough to *Glow* with respect to your skills, attitudes, and habits?" My suggestion is that you should glance at these ten questions every week. You can download them from the Hot Spots Movement Web site (http://www.hotspotsmovement.com) and pin them on your wall. After each question, you will see the specific actions related to that question. Look back at these actions if you need inspiration.

The second set of questions asks, "Are your colleagues and team doing enough to provide a context in which you can *Glow*?" Sit down and review these every month—preferably with the rest of your team. Again, after each question are listed the specific actions the question refers to.

The third set of questions asks, "Is the wider community or company in which you work doing enough to create a context in which you can *Glow*?" Again, review these every month to be sure that you are doing enough to create a wider context in which you can *Glow*.

The Glow Checklists

Personal *Glow* Checklist (Review Weekly)

Questions to Ask	Actions You Might Take
1. Could I work with people in a more trusting and cooperative way and increase my conversational and listening skills?	1.2, 1.3, 2.1, 2.3, 2.4, 2.5, 5.7
2. Can I do more to broaden my knowledge base?	7.1, 7.2, 7.3
3. Could I do more to create more time for reflection and the unexpected?	4.7, 5.3, 5.4, 5.5, 7.4, 7.5, 7.6, 7.7, 8.2
4. Is there more I can do to connect with my values?	8.3, 9.4
5. Is there more I can do to acknowledge and celebrate the differences between people?	4.2, 5.7
6. Should I do more to extend my networks beyond the boundaries of my acquaintances?	4.3, 5.7, 6.1, 6.2, 6.3, 6.4
7. Can I do more to add value to my communities of practice?	5.1, 5.2, 6.5
8. Is there more I could do to keep asking the important questions and demonstrate the conviction of my ideas?	2.2, 2.6, 8.1, 8.3, 8.4
9. Is there more I can do to craft exciting and meaningful tasks?	9.1, 9.2, 9.3, 9.4, 9.5, 9.6
10. Could I be more forceful about *Glowing*?	2.7, 7.7

Team *Glow* Checklist (Review Monthly)

Questions to Ask	Actions You Might Take
11. Is there more we could do to encourage people to trust and cooperate with each other and be welcoming and appreciative of others?	1.3, 1.4, 1.5, 5.7
12. Could we do more to encourage team members to make commitments with each other and make efforts to understand the context of their work?	1.7, 9.6
13. Is there more that my colleagues and I could do to introduce each other to people in their networks?	1.1, 1.2, 6.2
14. What more could we do to encourage each other to meet people from different businesses, functions, and companies?	6.3
15. What more can I do to ensure that our extended networks are welcomed into the team?	4.4, 4.5, 5.7
16. Are we listening carefully to what each other has to say and appreciating each other's ideas?	5.7, 7.1
17. What more can we do to engage in conversations and encourage people to ask the big questions?	2.3, 2.4, 7.3, 8.1
18. Could we do more to show excitement and openness to new ideas?	7.1, 7.3, 8.4
19. What efforts can we undertake together to make our work more meaningful?	9.1, 9.2, 9.6
20. Are we becoming overscheduled? If so, what can we do as a group to allow for greater serendipity?	7.4. 7.8. 8.2

Community or Business *Glow* Checklist (Review Monthly)

QUESTIONS TO ASK	ACTIONS YOU MIGHT TAKE
21. Could I do more to encourage senior executives to model cooperative behavior?	1.8
22. Am I encouraging leaders to mentor me and give me their time?	1.8
23. Can I do more to encourage executives to introduce me to their broader networks?	6.1, 6.2
24. What more can I do to encourage this organization to support people joining communities of practice?	5.1, 5.2
25. Is this company communicating a vision of the future that I find engaging and meaningful, and if not, what am I going to do about it?	8.1, 8.4
26. Are there projects and tasks at my job that resonate with my values, and if not, how might I go about creating ones that do?	8.3
27. Do we have enough forums for debate and questioning, and if not, how might I establish new ones?	2.6, 7.3, 8.1
28. Does this organization give me time to work on my own dreams, and if not, how am I going to make time for doing so?	5.4, 5.5, 7.5, 7.7
29. Is this company capable of creating meaningful work? How can I ensure that it does?	9.1, 9.2, 9.3
30. If this is the wrong place for me, how can I be sure my next job will help me *Glow*?	3.1, 3.2, 3.3, 6.8, 6.9, 6.10

Recommended Reading

A great many writers have influenced my thinking while developing the ideas expressed in *Glow* and in my earlier book, *Hot Spots*. An extensive bibliography can be found in that book; additional works that I have found of great value are presented here, organized, like this book, according to the components of the *Glow* Profile.

Cooperative Mindset

The whole idea of cooperation sits at the center of an exciting emerging field of research called positive psychology. My hunch is that over the next decade we will see a significant swing toward what I might call complex cooperation. So if you want to stay ahead of the curve, you may want to explore the following works.

David Bohm. *On Dialogue.* Ed. Lee Nichol. New York: Routledge, 1996.

> This book is not for the fainthearted, but if you want to dip into the mind of one of the great scholars of conversation and dialogue, here is where to start.

Kim S. Cameron, Jane E. Dutton, and Robert E. Quinn (eds.). *Positive Organizational Scholarship: Foundations of a New Discipline.* San Francisco: Berrett-Koehler, 2003.

Three professors at Michigan University have brought together a fascinating collection of ideas in this book. Many are pertinent not just to cooperation but also to jumping across worlds. Cameron and Dutton are key members of a community of practice in the relative new field of positive psychology.

Jane E. Dutton. *Energize Your Workplace: How to Create and Sustain High-Quality Connections at Work.* San Francisco: Jossey-Bass, 2003.

This is an interesting and insightful book about trust and cooperation, placed firmly in the context of work.

Theodore Zeldin. *Conversation: How Talk Can Change Our Lives.* Mahwah, N.J.: Hidden Spring, 1998, 2000.

This is a tiny and rather exquisite book about conversation sprinkled with pictures and ideas. It's a great book to have on hand when you need uplifting and want to embark on creative dialogue.

Jumping Across Worlds

Networks and their analysis are getting a great deal of academic attention right now, and some practitioners are embracing the ideas. I believe this is a development that you should keep an eye on.

Wayne E. Baker. *Achieving Success Through Social Capital: Tapping the Hidden Resources in Your Personal and Business Networks.* San Francisco: Jossey-Bass, 2000.

If you are interested in building your networks, this book provides a series of exercises that can help you understand where you are now and how to plot a course of action to where you want to be.

Rob Cross and Andrew Parker. *The Hidden Power of Social Networks: Understanding How Work Really Gets Done in Organizations.* Boston: Harvard Business School Press, 2004.

The authors look at networks primarily from the perspective of organizations. The book contains many useful examples of network diagrams and is particularly helpful in its discussion of how knowledge travels around networks.

Martin Kilduff and Wenpin Tsai. *Social Networks and Organizations.* Thousand Oaks, Calif.: Sage, 2003.

This is a fairly scholarly book in which the authors take an overview of the field of networks from various perspectives. It contains a useful list of recommended reading selections if you are inclined to dig deeper into this fascinating emerging field.

Scott E. Page. *The Difference: How the Power of Diversity Creates Better Groups, Firms, Schools, and Societies.* Princeton, N.J.: Princeton University Press, 2007.

If heuristics fascinate you, this is the book from which to learn more about them. Page is a professor of complex systems who has shown that progress and innovation depend less on the lone thinker and more on diverse people working together and capitalizing on their individuality.

Bertrand Russell. *The Conquest of Happiness.* London: Allen & Unwin, 1930.

If you liked his quote in Chapter Eleven on friendship and strangers, you may want to dip into the book from which it was taken.

Etienne Wenger, Richard McDermott, and William N. Snyder. *Cultivating Communities of Practice: A Guide to Managing Knowledge.* Boston: Harvard Business School Press, 2002.

This book takes a thoughtful and highly practical approach to communities of practice. If Action 5, jumping out of the boundaries that constrain you, is an area you feel you need to work on, I suggest you take a closer look at this book. It contains detailed case studies of communities and many fascinating insights about how they can flourish and the dangers they face.

Igniting Latent Energy

There are a great many books on vision and development; this is a rather idiosyncratic mix of books that have inspired me.

Mihaly Csikszentmihalyi. *Finding Flow: The Psychology of Engagement with Everyday Life*. New York: Basic Books, 1997.

> Creating meaningful, fulfilling work is an exciting challenge for all of us. This book concentrates on what it would take for you to create a working context that inspires you. He uses the notion of "flow" to suggest times and occasions when you are truly and wholly engaged in your work.

Herminia Ibarra. *Working Identity: Unconventional Strategies for Reinventing Your Career*. Boston : Harvard Business School Press, 2003.

> Ibarra has some fascinating things to say about how to shape a meaningful working life. Her argument is that changing yourself and your work is less about reflection and more about doing. Like me, she believes that watching others and modeling their behavior is key to personal change. So her emphasis is on getting yourself into places where people are doing what you would like to be doing.

Joseph Jaworski. *Synchronicity: The Inner Path of Leadership*. San Francisco: Berrett-Koehler, 1996.

> There are many inspiring stories about how a person found his or her voice and vision. This is one of the best. Jaworski's focus is on deepening one's understanding of reality and shaping the future. What is inspiring about this book is how the author has made space in his life for the unexpected to emerge.

Thomas W. Malone. *The Future of Work: How the New Order of Business Will Shape Your Organization, Your Management Style, and Your Life.* Boston: Harvard Business School Press, 2004.

Crafting visions and asking igniting questions can be supported by a deeper understanding of the future. There are many futurologists around; my personal favorite is Tom Malone at MIT. He provides an extensive and far-reaching view of how work will evolve over the coming decades.

Peter Schwartz. *The Art of the Long View: Planning for the Future in an Uncertain World.* New York: Currency/Doubleday, 1991.

Peter Schwartz is one of a group of people that includes Arie de Geus, Pierre Wack, and Kees van der Heijden, who developed the art of scenario planning. In this book he describes how he as a futurist at the Royal Dutch Shell Group worked on developing the scenarios the group used in the 1990s.

About the Author

 For thirty years, Lynda Gratton has been fascinated by work. Her thinking, writing, and consulting have focused on three interwoven strands: individuals, teams, and organizations. This book has provided a wonderful opportunity to bring all three strands together.

Lynda began by developing the first strand through a profound interest in people. Trained initially as a psychologist with a doctorate in motivation theory, she has since coached executives and students to become more energized and innovative. Many of the stories and some of the tools in *Glow* have been developed by working with her students and executives. In 2007 Lynda became the founding director of the Centre for Women in Business at London Business School. In working with women around the world, she has gained real insight into some of the rewards of "jumping across worlds."

The second strand of work has been Lynda's engagement with teams. With her colleagues she has built one of the most significant data sets on innovation and teams and is an expert in virtual team working. Her work on teams has been published in *Harvard Business Review,* the *Sloan Management Review* (where she was awarded Best Article of 2003), the *Wall Street Journal,* and the

Economist. Lynda brings her insights into teams into this book through her experience with networks and working across boundaries.

Lynda's third strand of interest is her work with corporate senior executives and CEOs to show them how to create more vibrant and more innovative companies. In this respect she is considered one of the most influential thinkers in business. In 2007 the London *Times* ranked her as one of the top twenty thinkers in the world, and in 2008 the *Financial Times* selected her as the business thinker most likely to make a real difference over the next decade.

Lynda is Professor of Management Practice at London Business School and is the founder of the Hot Spots Movement. She has written six books and numerous articles. Her books have been translated into more than fifteen languages and are seen as seminal pieces in the field of corporate and individual development.

Over the past decade Lynda has been profiled in numerous publications, including *Personnel Today,* the *Guardian,* and the *Financial Times.* In 2007 *Human Resources* magazine ranked her as one of the top two most influential people in the profession. Over the past five years she has taken her message about energy and innovation to conferences in many parts of the world, including Australia, Austria, Estonia, Finland, Germany, India, Japan, the Netherlands, Singapore, and the United States.

Lynda lives in London and Spain with her two sons. You can visit her Web site at http://www.lyndagratton.com.

About the
Hot Spots Movement

Lynda Gratton founded the Hot Spots Movement in 2006. Since then, the movement has become the focus of a global community of many thousands of people, all of whom share a passion for bringing energy and innovation to people at work.

The core members of the team of the Hot Spots Movement are engaged in four areas of activity:

They conduct research in the field of energy and innovation. These research projects often bridge between academics and practicing managers to create insights and ideas that are robust and useful. Past research topics have included the leadership style most appropriate for leading complex teams and how virtual teams work together. You can find the current research agenda at http://www.hotspotsmovement.com.

They design and build world-class diagnostic profiles. These profiles enable people to create a deep awareness of what actions they should take now to significantly increase the energy and innovation in their work life, on their teams, and in their communities and organizations. The core team also runs an accreditation program to train profilers. You can look at the diagnostics profiles they have developed and see how to become an accredited profiler at http://www.hotspotsmovement.com.

They create virtual learning experiences. These learning activities include the "sixty-day learning journey," which is tailored to meet the specific development needs of teams and is delivered in a virtual environment. You can learn more at http://www.hotspotsmovement.com.

They train people world-wide in how to support and lead high-performing and innovative teams and communities. The flagship "Hotbed for Hot Spots" program runs in London every couple of months. There are also specialized programs to train human resource professionals and team leaders.

These programs are often run inside companies, and the core team conducts accreditation programs to train trainers. To learn more about these programs or to learn how to become an accredited trainer, go to http://www.hotspotsmovement.com.

Index

Page numbers in *italics* indicate illustrations

READ ON ...

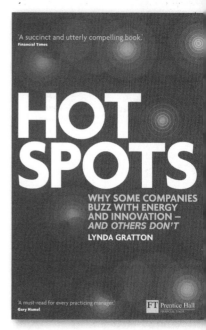

HOT
SPOTS

WHY SOME COMPANIES BUZZ
WITH ENERGY AND INNOVATION
– AND OTHERS DON'T

ISBN: 9780273711469

Why do some companies and teams buzz with energy, innovation and creativity? Why do these flares of activity occur in some companies and teams, and not in others?

This ground-breaking book from management guru Lynda Gratton addresses just these questions. It is based on extensive research with industry leaders such as BP, Nokia, Adidas, Linux, Goldman Sachs, Ogilvy One, Unilever and Reuters. Gratton explores the conditions and environments that are conducive to the creation of Hot Spots, and in doing so, she offers you a range of invaluable tools for achieving higher levels of effectiveness and productivity than you ever thought possible.

'A must-read for every practicing manager.' **Gary Hamel**

'Just about the worst affliction a company can suffer from is sluggishness. In Hot Spots, *Lynda Gratton prescribes the antidote.'*
Sir Martin Sorrell, CEO, WPP

'A must-read for anyone keen to move from the 'Big Freeze' of inertia to the energy of Hot Spots.' **Tom Glocer, CEO, Reuters Group PLC**